SPECIAL REPORT 248

# *Shopping for Safety*

## Providing Consumer Automotive Safety Information

*Committee for Study of*
*Consumer Automotive Safety Information*

TRANSPORTATION RESEARCH BOARD
National Research Council

National Academy Press
Washington, D.C. 1996

# TRANSPORTATION RESEARCH BOARD SPECIAL REPORT 248

Subscriber Category
IVB safety and human performance

Transportation Research Board publications are available by ordering directly from TRB. They may also be obtained on a regular basis through organizational or individual affiliation with TRB; affiliates or library subscribers are eligible for substantial discounts. For further information, write to the Transportation Research Board, National Research Council, 2101 Constitution Avenue, N.W., Washington, D.C. 20418.

NOTICE: The project that is the subject of this report was approved by the Governing Board of the National Research Council, whose members are drawn from the councils of the National Academy of Sciences, the National Academy of Engineering, and the Institute of Medicine. The members of the committee responsible for the report were chosen for their special competencies and with regard for appropriate balance.

This report has been reviewed by a group other than the authors according to the procedures approved by a Report Review Committee consisting of members of the National Academy of Sciences, the National Academy of Engineering, and the Institute of Medicine.

The study was sponsored by the National Highway Traffic Safety Administration of the U.S. Department of Transportation.

## LIBRARY OF CONGRESS CATALOGING-IN-PUBLICATION DATA

National Research Council (U.S.). Committee for Study of Consumer Automotive Safety Information.
    Shopping for safety : providing consumer automotive safety information / Committee for Study of Consumer Automotive Safety Information, Transportation Research Board, National Research Council.
        p.   cm. — (Special report / Transportation Research Board, National Research Council ; 248)
    ISBN 0-309-06209-8
    1. Automobiles—Crashworthiness.   2. Automobiles—Defects—Reporting.   3. Consumer education.   I. Title.   II. Series: Special report (National Research Council (U.S.). Transportation Research Board) ; 248.
TL242.N38   1996
381'.45629222—dc20                                                      96-11131
                                                                          CIP

*Cover design:* Karen L. White

# PREFACE

Mindful of growing consumer interest in motor vehicle safety features and the federal role in providing consumer automotive safety information, Congress requested an independent study of consumer information needs by the National Academy of Sciences. The Conference Committee Report authorizing the study recognized that the National Highway Traffic Safety Administration (NHTSA) already provides information to consumers on the crashworthiness of vehicles in frontal collisions. However, the information is limited in scope and does not provide a comprehensive assessment of a vehicle's likely overall safety performance. Hence the request for a study, sponsored by NHTSA, that would broadly examine motor vehicle consumer safety information needs and the most cost-effective methods of communicating this information to the public.

Growth of the consumer movement in the 1960s and 1970s led to the introduction of information regulations in the belief that incomplete or inaccurate information about product attributes and risks can distort consumer choices and lessen the incentives for firms to produce safer products. Information labels and hazard warnings proliferated on consumer products ranging from household chemical cleaners to food products to major appliances.

In theory, more complete information should foster more informed purchase decisions, at the same time allowing for individual differences in preferences and risk aversion. In practice, the results have been mixed. Information is effective to the extent that consumers perceive it as important and are able to process and use the message conveyed. Thus this study examines what vehicle safety information should be developed for consumers. It also addresses how the information should be structured and communicated and how a process can be put in place that promotes continuing improvements in consumer information and safer vehicle designs.

To conduct the study, the Transportation Research Board (TRB) formed a panel of nine members under the leadership of M. Granger Morgan, Head of the Department of Engineering and Public Policy at

Carnegie-Mellon University. The committee includes experts in motor vehicle and highway safety, highway safety data, consumer education and information, risk communication, information regulation and public policy, product evaluation, and product development and manufacturing. Panel members, who are drawn from universities, highway safety organizations, the insurance industry, and consumer groups, reached consensus on all the report findings and recommendations.

The committee wishes to acknowledge the work of many individuals and organizations who contributed to the report, in particular those who participated in a 1-day workshop held early in the committee's deliberations.[1] The workshop, which responded to congressional concerns that the committee obtain the views of a wide array of experts, from industry to consumer and safety advocates, addressed motor vehicle safety information needs and public perceptions of safety in automobile purchase decisions. Special thanks are expressed to Eva Kasten, Executive Vice President of the Advertising Council, Inc., who provided the committee with information about public advertising strategies and moderated one of the workshop sessions.

Nancy P. Humphrey managed the study and drafted major portions of the final report under the guidance of the committee and the supervision of Stephen R. Godwin, Director of Studies and Information Services. Suzanne Schneider, Assistant Executive Director of TRB, managed the report review process. In accordance with the National Research Council report review procedures, the report was reviewed by an independent group of reviewers.

The final report was edited and prepared for publication under the supervision of Nancy A. Ackerman, Director of Reports and Editorial Services, TRB. Special appreciation is expressed to Norman Solomon, who edited the report; to Rona Briere, who helped reorganize sections of the report, and to Marguerite Schneider, who assisted in meetings, logistics, and communications with the committee and provided word processing support for numerous drafts.

## NOTE

1. The workshop agenda, including speakers, is included as Appendix A.

# CONTENTS

# EXECUTIVE SUMMARY

The purpose of this study is to examine consumer needs for automotive safety information and the most cost-effective and meaningful methods of communicating this information. Current programs and the need for a process to support continuing improvement of consumer vehicle safety information and thereby provide additional incentives for manufacturers to enhance vehicle safety are addressed. The focus is primarily on development of better safety information for new car purchasers, particularly safety-conscious consumers.

## MOTOR VEHICLE CRASH AVOIDANCE AND CRASHWORTHINESS

Automobile crashes are complex events that result from the interaction of driver behavior, the driving environment (e.g., weather, time of day, type of road), and vehicle design. Experts agree that driver error or inappropriate driver behavior—drunk and reckless driving—is the dominant factor affecting the likelihood of being in a crash. Human characteristics, such as age and state of health, also affect the likelihood of surviving crash injuries.

The dominance of the human factor in crash causation does not diminish the important effect of vehicle design and safety features on crash likelihood or, in particular, on crash outcomes. Drivers cannot change their age or control the driving behavior of others, but they can decide which vehicle to buy and attempt to select the safest vehicle that will meet their needs and minimize crash likelihood and injury potential.

Vehicle features affect safety in two ways: (*a*) they help the driver avoid a crash or recover from a driving error (crash avoidance) and (*b*)

1

they provide protection from harm during a crash (crashworthiness). Characteristics such as vehicle stability and braking performance affect the probability of being in a crash, all else being equal. But the driver plays a more important role in determining the extent to which these crash avoidance features reduce crash likelihood. For example, the high fatality rates for drivers of sports cars—vehicles noted for their low center of gravity and stability as well as advanced handling and braking capabilities—attest to the importance of driver and use patterns, which largely determine crash involvement. Once in a crash, however, vehicle characteristics that contribute to crashworthiness, such as size and weight, how the vehicle absorbs energy, and restraint system attributes, play a large role in determining the likelihood and extent of occupant injury.

Because of the close coupling of vehicle characteristics and vehicle crashworthiness, the motor vehicle safety research program of the National Highway Traffic Safety Administration (NHTSA) has given top priority to research on measures for improving vehicle crashworthiness. Many standards have been developed and injury mitigation measures introduced, such as air bags, which have been incorporated into most new vehicles. These programs are the source of much of the comparative information about vehicle safety features and performance available to consumers.

## Current Consumer Automotive Safety Information

Considerable information is available to consumers about vehicle safety. NHTSA, the agency with statutory authority to provide consumer automotive safety information, makes available comparative data on the crashworthiness of vehicles in the same class from full-frontal crash tests conducted in its New Car Assessment Program; the insurance industry publishes information about injury claims and death rates by vehicle make and model and recently has provided comparative data on vehicle crashworthiness in offset frontal crash tests, representing a more common type of frontal crash; manufacturers advertise the safety features of their vehicles; and Consumers Union, publisher of *Consumer Reports*, runs tests of such vehicle safety characteristics as emergency handling and braking performance. Consumers Union and, more recently, NHTSA and the Insurance Institute for Highway Safety have attempted to compile comparative vehicle safety information in consumer-oriented publications. Thus, some information on vehicle safety is available to help consumers comparison shop.

Current safety information, however, has several limitations:

◆ The information is incomplete and difficult for consumers to pull together in any summary assessment and comparison of the overall performance of different vehicles.

◆ Current crash test results can be compared only among vehicles in the same size and weight class. The results do not reflect the inherent advantage of heavier cars or the fact that larger cars are more likely to have additional crush space to protect the integrity of the occupant compartment in more severe crashes.

◆ The repeatability of crash test results is an issue. Only one test per vehicle is conducted because of the cost of testing. Thus the range of variance in test scores is not well established, and the uncertainties of the results are not acknowledged in the published scores.

◆ Finally, current crash tests, which are focused on frontal crashes, do not provide a comprehensive picture of vehicle crashworthiness given the real-world variation in crash configurations and speeds. (Crash test performance, while an important indicator of vehicle crashworthiness, is unlikely ever to be highly correlated with real-world crash outcomes, which reflect driver characteristics and where, when, and how much the vehicle is driven.) Actual crash data on fatalities and injury claims by vehicle make and model reflect real crash experience. However, it is difficult to separate the vehicle from driver characteristics in communicating to consumers how the vehicle, as opposed to the driver and the roadway environment, contributes to crash occurrence and injury outcomes.

In summary, advances have been made in understanding vehicle safety, particularly how vehicles perform in crashes and the mechanisms that cause injury. Some of this information has been made available to consumers in a form that enables comparisons of vehicle safety features and characteristics, but much more could be done to make the information useful.

## CONSUMER DECISION-MAKING AND SAFETY INFORMATION REQUIREMENTS

To be most effective, consumer safety information should be based on a systematic understanding of what consumers know about vehicle safety and how they go about obtaining and using information in making automobile purchase decisions. Research should be conducted on what people know and believe about automobile safety and how they think about safety in selecting among different types of vehicles as an important step in developing improved consumer automotive safety information. Such research, which should be undertaken by NHTSA, is neither conceptually difficult nor expensive.

Market surveys suggest the existence of a growing safety-conscious market segment of new car purchasers. Yet it is unclear what consumers understand about safety—whether they equate safety with the presence of specific features like air bags, or whether they also have an understanding of the more basic factors that affect vehicle performance in a crash, like vehicle weight and size. Nor is it clear how they incorporate safety information in making automobile purchase decisions. The available survey data suggest that safety considerations are used most often to help narrow choices among specific makes and models once consumers have decided on a general type of vehicle on the basis of intended use, budget constraints, and other preferences. A better understanding of what consumers believe or understand about vehicle safety and how and when they think about safety in choosing a vehicle is important to the design of a communication that is relevant and useful to the consumer.

Once the context and content of the information are more clearly defined, determining how best to communicate and disseminate it is also a matter for empirical study. Information is likely to be considered if it is simple to acquire and use and is provided at the appropriate time. The limited information that is available, which must be confirmed by more systematic studies by NHTSA, suggests that consumers would like a standardized comprehensive vehicle safety rating applied to all passenger vehicles, independent sources of information (e.g., the government), and information made available early in the search process—not just at the point of sale.

## KEY FINDINGS AND RECOMMENDATIONS

### Findings

On the basis of a review of knowledge about vehicle safety characteristics, crash likelihood, and injury causation as well as the information currently available to consumers, the committee reached the following conclusions:

◆ Considerable information about vehicle safety characteristics and features is available to consumers, but it is not always timely, accessible, or in a form that readily supports comparison shopping.

◆ Several steps could be taken in the short term to address these limitations (see recommendations).

◆ In the long term, summary measures of vehicle safety would help consumers incorporate safety in new vehicle purchase decisions.

◆ At present, development of a defensible summary measure of *vehicle crashworthiness* is feasible only if current knowledge is supplemented with expert judgment. The uncertainties of present knowledge preclude development of a measure constructed strictly on scientific grounds, but, in the committee's judgment, the relation between vehicle characteristics and occupant protection is sufficiently strong that a useful measure of crashworthiness can be developed if expert judgment is used and the uncertainties are acknowledged. The most reliable estimates can probably be achieved if experts begin with information about the relation between crashworthiness and vehicle weight and size, and then use analysis combined with their expert professional judgment to incorporate results from crash tests, highway crash statistics, and a variety of other factors, such as the presence or absence of specific design features. Over time the estimates can be improved by development of more field-relevant crash tests and test criteria, more reliable test dummies, and collection of more comparable and consistent field accident data.

◆ The state of knowledge is not well enough advanced, even with expert judgment, to develop a corresponding summary measure for *crash avoidance*. A major problem is the limited role that vehicle characteristics (as opposed to driving behavior) currently play in predicting crash likelihood. However, with many vehicle technology improvements (e.g., collision avoidance systems) in development, crash avoidance features may play a larger role in the future, and continuing attention to this area is merited.

## Recommendations

On the basis of these findings, the committee recommends the following measures to improve the provision of automotive safety information to consumers.

## Improvements to Existing Information

In the short term, the following measures would improve the automotive safety information available to consumers:

- ◆ Consumers could be provided with more explicit information on
  —The importance of vehicle size and weight in crash outcomes,
  —The benefits of proper use of vehicle safety features such as occupant restraint systems and antilock brakes,
  —The frequency of crash types for which crash test results are available, and
  —The uncertainties associated with crash test results.
- ◆ The reliability of crash test results should be established and the sources of variance identified.
- ◆ The presentation and dissemination of existing vehicle safety information could be improved by increasing awareness that the information is available and by making it more accessible.

## Development of Summary Measures

In the longer term, new summary measures could be developed to provide consumers with comparative safety information on overall vehicle performance that is more helpful than current data in making purchase decisions. The following recommendations indicate how development of summary measures could be accomplished:

- ◆ From the consumers' perspective, one overall measure that combines the relative importance of vehicle crashworthiness and crash avoidance features would be ideal. However, for the foreseeable future, summary measures of crashworthiness and crash avoidance should be presented separately because of differences in the current level of knowledge and in the roles of the vehicle and the driver in the two areas. An effort to develop a summary measure of crashworthiness should go forward, incorporating defensible information supplemented with the professional judgment of automotive experts, statisticians, and decision analysts and reflecting the range of uncertainty associated with those judgments. For now, a checklist of safety features related to crash avoidance rather than a summary measure is recommended.
- ◆ Because consumers differ in the amount of detail they want and can manage, communication of new vehicle safety measures can best be

accomplished through a hierarchically organized approach. The most highly summarized information should be provided on a vehicle label that includes a simple graphical display of comparative crashworthiness performance and a checklist of crash avoidance features. Product labels, such as the energy efficiency label for major appliances and the fuel economy label on passenger vehicles, provide model formats that consumers have found useful and easy to understand. Because of the amount of information already provided on vehicle window stickers—price, fuel economy, vehicle features—a separate label is desirable for all vehicle safety-related information. It may be necessary to display the summary safety information in some other prominent location because of limitations on window space for some vehicles and concerns about visibility in driving test vehicles. An accompanying brochure would contain more detailed explanations of the summary measures, the assumptions used in their calculation, and their key components such as vehicle size and weight. A handbook would provide complete comparisons among vehicles. These materials should be developed, tested, and refined with groups of typical users.

◆ A multichannel approach is recommended for dissemination of vehicle safety information. Consumers need safety information to assist decision making well before they reach the dealer, and product labels are more effective if they are part of an overall communications strategy. A mix of dissemination outlets is suggested, including NHTSA's safety hotline and the Internet, insurance industry and automobile club mailings, and reprints in consumer journals. Development of a segment for driver education courses on purchasing a safe car, and of course public service advertising, should help increase awareness of the label and backup materials.

Before these steps are taken, preliminary research into consumer decision making and safety information requirements should be undertaken by NHTSA. Such research should address

◆ How consumers conceptualize automotive safety,

◆ How consumers apply safety information in selecting among vehicle types and specific models, and

◆ How automotive safety information can best be communicated and disseminated to consumers.

## Development of a Process To Stimulate Better Consumer Safety Information and Safer Cars

Finally, there are a number of organizational considerations that must be addressed in any effort to develop the measures outlined.

Development of summary measures of vehicle safety for consumers should not be viewed as an end in itself but rather as part of a continuing long-term process to yield both better consumer information and safer cars. The Secretary of the Department of Transportation (DOT) should encourage automobile manufacturers and the insurance industry, among others, to join NHTSA in a voluntary effort to achieve these goals. Congress should initiate the process with a formal request and appropriate funding, charging DOT to ensure the development by 2000 of reliable summary vehicle safety measures and a mechanism for continuing improvements. The secretary would issue a progress report to Congress in 18 months and determine the most appropriate organizational structure to carry the program forward. If for any reason the voluntary process reaches a stalemate, legislative action would be necessary.

Two organizational approaches to oversee the process were identified as most desirable: (a) establishment of a federal advisory committee and (b) creation of a public-private Automotive Safety Institute (ASI). The functions of the two organizations would be the same— development of improved vehicle safety information, including summary safety measures, and dissemination strategies. They would also develop a program of long-term applied research leading to advances in crash testing, design procedures, and vehicle technologies to yield better safety measures and safer automobile designs. With a NHTSA-appointed advisory committee, the process could start quickly with a modest annual investment of $1 million to $2 million and NHTSA staff support. The ASI approach, which would involve a partnership between NHTSA, the automobile manufacturers selling in the U.S. market, and the insurance industry, probably offers the best chance of achieving a sustained long-term program. However, a new institute would be more difficult to establish and could cost more. Under either alternative, a fully operational program of research and vehicle testing and design initiatives would require annual resources of $10 million to $20 million or more, most of which could be expected to come from participating industries.

## BENEFITS OF CONSUMER AUTOMOTIVE SAFETY INFORMATION

A program to improve consumer vehicle safety information would have many benefits. Meaningful comparative information that is widely accessible and easy to obtain and use can provide a powerful market stimulus influencing consumer choice and manufacturer design of safer vehicles, ultimately reducing the number of fatalities and injuries. With about 15 million new passenger vehicles sold each year, there is a large potential market for clear and understandable comparative safety information. Moreover, automobile manufacturers would have an incentive to design safety improvements so their products receive good ratings on summary safety measures. Manufacturers would also benefit from a program with the potential to integrate crash test with safety information requirements and from the increased demand of more safety-conscious consumers for new cars with the most advanced safety features. The insurance industry would benefit from any reduction in claims arising from crashes. Finally, the value of even a small decline in net fatalities that could be attributed to a consumer automotive safety information program could be considerable, and, in the committee's judgment, might easily exceed the costs of supplying better information to consumers and vehicle designers. For example, using current estimates of the public's willingness to pay to reduce the risk of death in a motor vehicle crash, a $20 million per year program of research and information would only need to achieve a net mortality reduction on the order of 10 deaths per year to justify program expenditures.

# 1

# INTRODUCTION AND OVERVIEW

$M$otor vehicle crashes are the leading cause of accidental death and a major cause of unintentional injury in the United States. They burden society with nearly \$140 billion in annual economic losses alone (NHTSA 1995, i).[1] Although the current fatality rate of 1.1 fatalities per 100 million vehicle kilometers (1.7 fatalities per 100 million vehicle miles) traveled is a historic low, it nonetheless represents more than 40,000 annual deaths and 3 million injuries (NHTSA 1995, i). Federal motor vehicle safety standards and vehicle design improvements, which resulted in the introduction of such safety features as air bags, have played an important role in improving highway safety. Fatality rates have fallen by nearly 70 percent since 1966, the year federal motor vehicle safety standards were authorized (NHTSA 1995).

Past safety gains notwithstanding, consumers have become more aware of the value of vehicle safety features and rate them as important factors in passenger vehicle purchasing decisions. Consumers could make even more informed purchase decisions with accurate comparative information on vehicle safety characteristics. Over time, improved comparative data on vehicle safety characteristics could also affect vehicle design as manufacturers respond to market pressure to provide safer vehicles. In addition, consumer safety information can be an appropriate complement to regulation: within a set of minimum standards, it enables consumers to make choices that reflect individual preferences and attitudes toward risk (Magat and Viscusi 1992, 4).

The purpose of this study is to examine consumer automotive safety information requirements and the most cost-effective methods of communicating this information. More specifically, the congressional request that prompted the study asks for an evaluation of "the validity of current programs, public and private, in providing accurate information to consumers on the real-world safety of vehicles, the possibility of improving the system in a cost-effective and realistic manner, and the best methods of providing useful information to consumers" (Appendix B).

Experiences with other informational programs, such as energy efficiency labeling for major appliances and fuel economy information for passenger vehicles, suggest that clearly presented, meaningful information can raise awareness and, over time, foster more informed purchase decisions.

## LEGISLATIVE CONTEXT AND SCOPE OF STUDY

The National Highway Traffic Safety Administration (NHTSA) is the lead federal agency for motor vehicle regulation and for providing consumer automotive information.[2] Title II of the 1972 Motor Vehicle Information and Cost Savings Act (Public Law 92-513) directed NHTSA to develop comparative information on the damage susceptibility, crashworthiness, repairability, and insurance costs of individual makes and models of automobiles for distribution to consumers (Booz, Allen Applied Research 1976, II-1). The intent was to help consumers select wisely among purchase options and provide market incentives for vehicle manufacturers to produce cars that are less susceptible to damage, more crashworthy, and more easily repaired (U.S. Congress. Senate 1971, pp. 10, 15–16, 23–24; U.S. Congress. House 1972, pp. 7–8, 17–18).

NHTSA's primary response to the vehicle safety-related information requirements of Title II was to establish the New Car Assessment Program (NCAP) in 1978. The program provides consumers with a measure of the relative crashworthiness of passenger vehicles of similar weight by estimating injury levels of vehicle occupants involved in frontal crashes from crash tests using humanlike instrumented dummies. Test results, which were first made available for selected model year 1979 automobiles, have been published annually ever since. In response to a 1992 congressional request, NHTSA adopted a simplified, more user-friendly rating scheme to make the test results more understandable and accessible to consumers (NHTSA 1993, 8).

More recently, as part of a Notice of Proposed Rulemaking on rollover prevention (*Federal Register* 1994), NHTSA proposed a new consumer safety information requirement—a safety label on all passenger vehicles providing comparative information on their resistance to rollover.[3] Both the automobile industry and safety advocacy groups raised issues concerning the proposed measures of and the presentation of information about vehicle rollover propensity.[4] The desirability of the safety label itself is an issue. Because of various federal and state requirements, vehicles have, or will soon have, labels providing information on many subjects—fuel economy, domestic content, bumper impact capability, proper placement of child safety seats, and use of safety belts with air bags—as well as more traditional price and equipment information. Additional safety information could overwhelm the consumer or simply be ignored, lessening or eliminating the value of the information.

The reaction to NHTSA's proposed safety information requirement prompted Congress to request this study and delay issuance of a final rule until its completion. In response to these concerns, the study attempts to determine

- ◆ Appropriate safety-related characteristics for which consumer information is needed;
- ◆ The technical feasibility of developing simple and meaningful measures of complex safety information, including the feasibility of establishing summary measures of vehicle safety;
- ◆ Meaningful and cost-effective approaches of conveying safety and other automotive information to consumers; and
- ◆ Institutional strategies needed to promote continuing improvements in consumer safety information and vehicle design.

The study is focused on development of more meaningful vehicle safety information to foster better consumer purchase decisions. New vehicles, including passenger cars and light truck vehicles (i.e, pickup trucks, vans, and sport utility vehicles) are the primary focus, but some of the approaches could also be relevant for used cars.[5]

In the remainder of this chapter, some of the complexities involved in the development of meaningful consumer automotive safety information are introduced. These include the multidimensional nature of vehicle safety; the relative contribution of the vehicle, the driver, and the environment to crash likelihood; consumer attitudes toward the riskiness of driving generally; and institutional issues affecting information provision.

## WHAT IS VEHICLE SAFETY?

One of the difficulties of providing vehicle safety information in a simplified format for consumers is defining what is meant by vehicle safety. Unlike vehicle fuel economy or appliance energy efficiency, which can readily be represented in one or two summary measures (e.g., gas mileage in city driving and highway driving), vehicle safety is a multidimensional concept that is difficult to capture in a single measure.

One way to conceptualize vehicle safety is to distinguish vehicle design characteristics and features related to the probability of being in a crash—referred to as crash avoidance—from those providing protection from harm during a crash—referred to as crashworthiness.

### Crash Avoidance

Vehicle characteristics such as braking performance, vehicle stability, and visibility can help drivers avoid a crash or recover from a driving error. For example, antilock brakes prevent the wheels from locking and the car from skidding, thus helping the driver maintain control of the vehicle, particularly on wet and slippery surfaces (IIHS 1994b). Vehicles that have a low center of gravity relative to their track width have less of a propensity to roll over if the car runs off the road or collides with a barrier or another vehicle, all else being equal (Gillespie 1992, 310–313).

In some cases the potential benefits of crash avoidance features may be considerably muted by driver behavior. For example, sports cars, which are known for their stability and handling capabilities, have some of the highest fatality rates as a vehicle class (IIHS 1994c). In the future, new technologies under development as part of the Intelligent Transportation Systems program[6]—heads-up instrument display panels, enhanced night vision systems, and collision avoidance systems—may enhance driver ability to avoid crashes.

### Vehicle Crashworthiness

Once a crash occurs, vehicle safety characteristics such as weight and size play a critical role in determining the protection afforded vehicle occupants. The extent of injury is directly affected by the crash energy and the manner in which vehicle occupants experience the associated forces. Heavier vehicles typically have a larger interior space, thus providing a longer distance for the occupants to decelerate to a stop and reducing the likelihood of injury (Evans 1994, 12). Larger vehicles, with more external energy-absorbing structures, do a better job of preventing intrusion into the occupant compartment and increasing the time the crash forces take to reach the occupants (O'Neill 1995, 4, 6–7). All else being equal, occupants of a heavier, larger car will fare better than the occupants of a smaller, lighter car if the two cars collide.

Vehicle size and weight thus help mitigate the effects of a collision with another vehicle or an object outside the car. Occupant protection features have been developed to reduce what are known as the "second" and "third" collisions, that is, the collision of the vehicle occupants inside the car (against the dashboard or windshield) and the collision of internal organs within the human body, respectively. For example, collapsible steering columns and padded dashboards help deflect or cushion collision impacts. Safety belt systems, which are required in all vehicles, help avoid the second impact. The seat belt is intended to restrain the lower torso and help hold the occupant inside the vehicle, whereas the shoulder belt primarily keeps the upper body away from the steering wheel, dashboard, or windshield (IIHS 1994b). Air bags further protect the occupant's upper body in a severe frontal crash by providing an energy-absorbing cushion between the driver or front seat passenger and the interior of the vehicle (IIHS 1994b). Frontal air bags, however, provide no protection in rollovers or rear- or side-impact crashes; only safety belt systems offer this protection. Seat- and door-mounted air bags are now being introduced by some manufacturers to provide better protection in side-impact crashes.

This brief summary of how vehicle characteristics and features affect highway safety illustrates the complexity of attempting to describe these factors in a simple yet meaningful manner as a basis for comparing the relative safety of individual vehicles. A major issue, which is discussed in the following section, is the difficulty of isolating vehicle factors from driver behavior and environmental conditions, which all interact to affect crash likelihood and crash outcomes.

## CRASH CAUSATION AND THE ROLE OF VEHICLE-RELATED FACTORS

Vehicle crashes are complex events involving driver behavior, vehicle characteristics, and environmental conditions. Three in-depth studies of crashes dating from the 1970s (Perchonok 1972; Sabey 1973; Treat et al. 1979) attempted to assign causality to each of the major factors contributing to crash likelihood. The studies found that driver error or inappropriate driving behavior was the major contributing factor in 60 to 90 percent of motor vehicle crashes. Environmental factors (e.g., weather, road conditions, signing, and lighting) played a major role in 12 to 35 percent of the crashes. Vehicle-related factors (e.g., brake failures) were dominant in only 5 to 20 percent of the crashes.

A recent General Accounting Office (GAO) study (GAO 1994) also investigated the relative contributions of driver attributes and vehicle characteristics to crash likelihood.[7] GAO found that driver characteristics such as age and traffic violation history far outweighed vehicle factors—including vehicle age, weight, and size—in predicting crash involvement (GAO 1994, 2, 3). Thus, although vehicles differ in many of their characteristics and features, vehicle-related characteristics are only one factor, and to the extent prior studies are correct, a small factor in crash likelihood.

Once in a crash, however, vehicle characteristics that contribute to crashworthiness, such as size and weight, how the vehicle absorbs energy, and restraint system attributes, play a large role in determining the likelihood and extent of occupant injury. In fact, because of this close coupling of vehicle characteristics and vehicle crashworthiness, federal regulations and research have placed a high priority on measures for improving vehicle crashworthiness. Numerous studies have documented that crashworthiness improvements have resulted in measurable reductions in fatalities and that the benefits of crashworthiness regulations on the average are greater than the costs.[8]

## FEDERAL REGULATION OF VEHICLE SAFETY FEATURES

Nearly 30 years of federal safety regulation and manufacturer design to comply with these standards has resulted in great improvements in vehicle design and performance. In addition, safety regulations have provided standards against which individual vehicles can be compared and their performance measured.

The National Traffic and Motor Vehicle Safety Act (P.L. 89-563) of 1966 authorized the then newly created NHTSA to set minimum vehicle safety performance standards, which meet the needs of motor vehicle safety.[9] Within 2 years of its creation NHTSA had issued 29 motor vehicle safety standards and had proposed 95 more (Graham 1989, 32).

The primary concern of NHTSA's early vehicle-related programs was to improve vehicle crashworthiness in frontal crashes, because of the large number of fatalities and injuries in this type of crash (TRB 1990,

41). Early crashworthiness research focused on methods for reducing injury in frontal collisions through demonstration of air bag technologies and development of anthropometric test devices (crash dummies). These efforts culminated in Federal Motor Vehicle Safety Standard (FMVSS) 208 requiring that new automobiles not exceed certain injury thresholds measured in a 48-km/hr (30-mph) frontal crash test.[10]

After a lengthy and contentious debate over the technical feasibility and reliability of automatic or passive occupant restraint systems to improve vehicle crashworthiness, the U.S. Department of Transportation (DOT) issued a final rule in 1984 requiring automatic protection in new vehicles.[11] The automobile manufacturers could meet the amended FMVSS 208 with automatic safety belt systems or air bags; phase-in requirements began in model year 1987.

After the initial emphasis on mitigation of frontal collisions, NHTSA's attention shifted to occupant protection in side-impact crashes during the mid-1970s (TRB 1990, 41). After 10 years of development, NHTSA promulgated its amended regulation on side impact in 1988. The standard was upgraded in 1993 so that all passenger vehicles must now meet a dynamic side-impact crash standard.

In recent years NHTSA has focused on rollover crashes, another major source of fatalities and injuries (TRB 1990, 41). An Advance Notice of Proposed Rulemaking was published in January 1992, but NHTSA concluded in its recent Notice of Proposed Rulemaking that establishing a single minimum stability standard for passenger cars and light trucks could not be justified on cost-benefit grounds (*Federal Register* 1994, 33,258).[12] Instead, NHTSA is proposing a broad range of measures to address rollover crashes, including antilock brakes; increased roof strength, better window construction, and improved door latches; and the consumer safety label previously discussed (*Federal Register* 1994, 33,256).

Federal vehicle safety regulations appear to have contributed to greater uniformity in safety performance, particularly in vehicle crashworthiness as measured by frontal crash test results for passenger vehicles of roughly equivalent weight (Kahane et al. 1994). Moreover, safety standards now apply to all categories of vehicles. By 1998 all new passenger vehicles—light trucks, vans, and sport utility vehicles as well as cars—will be required to have the same major safety features and meet the same crash test standards.[13] (Appendix C gives the regulations that are or soon will be required for the passenger and light truck vehicle fleet.[14])

Federal vehicle safety standards also provide a source of comparative information about vehicle safety features and performance that can be adapted for consumer information purposes. Information is or soon will be available for a wide variety of vehicle safety characteristics and features, much of which is derived from vehicle regulatory requirements. However, some important vehicle safety characteristics, such as size, weight, energy-absorbing capability, and many nonregulated safety features are not reflected in federal motor vehicle safety standards.

## DRIVER ATTITUDES TO CRASH LIKELIHOOD AND VEHICLE SAFETY

There may be a receptive audience for vehicle safety information now that consumers have become more aware of the value of vehicle safety features. Some consumers, however, may take safety for granted in automobile purchasing decisions because of the existence of federal regulations. Participants in recent NHTSA focus groups gave credence to this possibility: "Safety is not going to be my prime concern because I know that by federal law there are certain features which must be on all vehicles. I trust those features" (S.W. Morris & Co. 1993, 20).

Consumer interest in vehicle safety information also may be affected by how drivers perceive the riskiness of driving. Millions of Americans drive each day and complete their trips safely, thus reinforcing the individual's perception that the risks involved in driving are low. With about 175 million licensed drivers, each driving an average of 21 400 km (13,400 mi) per year, the occurrence of a crash,[15] on the average, is one every 335 000 driver kilometers (209,400 driver miles) or every 16 years of driving. The occurrence of a fatality is considerably less—one every 93 million driver kilometers (58 million driver miles) or every 4,300 years of driving.[16] Of course, driving is not always conducted under average conditions. The likelihood of fatalities is considerably higher on two-lane rural roads, on weekend nights when alcohol consumption is a key factor, and for young (under 25) and older (65 or over) drivers and vehicle occupants. Nevertheless, the common perception, even among drivers who have been in a crash, is that such incidents are rare, unpredictable events largely outside reasonable human control—a view reinforced by the frequent direct feedback of crash-free motor vehicle trips (Evans 1991, 311).

Many drivers believe that driving risk is low and that they themselves are less likely than others to experience a crash. Research indicates that most drivers rank their own driving skills and safe driving practices as better than average (Evans 1991, 322–324; Williams et al. 1995, 119; Svenson 1981, 146). Thus, they may not be inclined to seek information on vehicle safety, or, where information is provided, they may view the information as applying to others.

## INSTITUTIONAL ISSUES

A final issue that affects the provision of meaningful consumer automotive safety information concerns the providers of that information. Congress has designated NHTSA as the lead agency with responsibility for this function, and NHTSA has enjoyed some success in this role. The agency's primary consumer vehicle safety information initiative—the NCAP—has encouraged manufacturers to design more crashworthy vehicles. Vehicle crash test scores have improved markedly since testing was begun in 1979, with the greatest improvements in the early 1980 model years. Parallel reductions in fatality likelihood for belted drivers in actual head-on collisions over this same period suggest that publication of NCAP scores contributed to vehicle design improvements (Kahane et al. 1994, 13).[17]

However, there are limitations to NHTSA's role as consumer safety information provider, suggesting the need for a broader-based effort. NHTSA's ability to develop more comprehensive consumer information is severely limited by resource constraints. Further progress also requires systematic rethinking of improvements in testing and measurement, which will be difficult for NHTSA if it does not have the collaboration of industry. Finally, safety is not the only policy objective for which NHTSA is responsible. For example, consumers could be urged to purchase larger and heavier cars to reduce the injury potential of vehicle occupants, but this prescription would likely be at odds with NHTSA's responsibility to improve vehicle fuel economy.

## IMPLICATIONS FOR STUDY

Given all the caveats about the difficulty of providing meaningful consumer automotive safety information—the multidimensional character of vehicle safety and crash likelihood, the diminishing variation in safety features among motor vehicles, and the low risk that many travelers assign to driving—why attempt to improve vehicle safety information? There are four good reasons. First, market incentives may not be adequate to provide the comprehensive safety information that consumers need to make informed purchase decisions. Second, although motor vehicle safety regulations have provided common safety standards among passenger vehicles, vehicles continue to differ in many safety-related dimensions (e.g., mass, size, stability, and crashworthiness). These dimensions can affect safety-related performance, which suggests the desirability of publicizing these differences. Third, the experience of NHTSA's NCAP indicates that providing comparative information on vehicle safety performance can be effective in motivating automobile manufacturers to build added safety into vehicle design. Fourth, the information may affect consumer attitudes and purchasing behavior. Many individuals of driving age will be in the market for a car[18] in the next few years, and market research suggests that consumers, at least new car purchasers, are more aware today of the value of vehicle safety features. Thus, a potentially large audience exists for meaningful vehicle safety information, which can help consumers select the safest vehicle that will meet their needs and minimize crash likelihood and injury potential.

## ORGANIZATION OF REPORT

The remainder of the report is concerned with what and how vehicle safety information should be provided to consumers. The key data sources and state of knowledge about vehicle crash avoidance and crashworthiness as a basis for providing consumer vehicle safety information are summarized in Chapter 2. The strengths and weaknesses of currently available consumer safety information are reviewed in Chapter 3, and recommendations are made for improving current information. An overview of what is known about how consumers think about automobile safety and how they search for and use information in making automobile purchase decisions is given in Chapter 4. Research to fill current gaps in knowledge is identified. Recommendations for developing and communicating improved consumer vehicle safety information, including summary measures of vehicle safety, are presented in Chapter 5, and an organizational structure and an implementation strategy to promote continuing improvements in consumer safety information and vehicle safety design are proposed in Chapter 6.

## NOTES

1. Economic costs include medical costs, present and future discounted earnings losses, legal and court costs, coroner or medical examiner costs, emergency services, insurance administrative expenses, and delay costs caused by the crash (NHTSA and FHWA 1991, 31). Costs are estimated in 1990 dollars.

2. However, other federal agencies are involved. The Environmental Protection Agency is responsible for fuel economy information, the Justice Department handles price labeling on new cars, and the Federal Trade Commission handles used car labeling.

3. In the longer run, the NHTSA-proposed safety label could contain other information on vehicle safety, such as vehicle performance in frontal and side-impact crashes. The Notice of Proposed Rulemaking indicated that NHTSA would propose such additions in a supplemental rulemaking (*Federal Register* 1994, 33,256).

4. Industry and safety advocates both criticized the proposed safety label, but for different reasons. The automobile manufacturers questioned the feasibility of providing meaningful comparative information on vehicle rollover propensity in a simplified form (AAMA 1994). Safety advocates supported the concept of a safety label but were highly critical of what they regard as the overly simplified information NHTSA currently provides on vehicle frontal crashworthiness (IIHS 1994a). Moreover, they strongly opposed the requirement of a safety label, perceiving it as a substitute for a rollover stability standard (Advocates for Highway and Auto Safety 1994).

5. Providing safety information about used vehicles is a far more complex task because of the potential for modifications to used vehicles as well as their different crash experience. However, some methods of communicating vehicle safety information on new vehicles (e.g., a safety brochure), depending on the information they include, could also be appropriate for used vehicles.

6. The Intelligent Transportation Systems program includes four major categories of technology: (*a*) advanced traffic management systems for controlling and optimizing traffic flows on road networks, (*b*) advanced traveler information systems, (*c*) advanced vehicle control systems, and (*d*) commercial vehicle operations (TRB 1991, 21–23).

7. The analysis was based on a North Carolina data base, and hence the findings cannot be generalized to the nation as a whole.

8. Evans (1991) summarizes the NHTSA estimates of fatality reductions for vehicle occupants that can be attributed to the introduction of individual crashworthiness regulations, which range from 0.33 percent to 4.4 percent, and estimates larger combined effects in the neighborhood of 11 percent. (Note that these results do not include effects on nonoccupants, who, it can be argued, are largely unaffected by crashworthiness measures that are aimed at protecting vehicle occupants, such as energy-absorbing steering

columns.) Other researchers such as Crandall et al. (1986) have found that "the total benefits from the lifesaving effects of [crashworthiness] safety regulation are substantially greater than the costs of the required safety features on passenger cars under most reasonable assumptions" (p. 84).

9. The companion Highway Safety Act (P.L. 89-564) of 1966 provided national standards to guide state and local highway safety programs and provided grants to support these activities.

10. Specifically, the test measures the force of impact on the heads, chests, and upper legs of electronically instrumented, safety-belted dummies in the driver and passenger seats.

11. DOT agreed to rescind the federal requirement that automobile manufacturers install air bags or automatic belts if states representing two-thirds of the population mandated the use of safety belts. In the end, however, the conditions laid out by DOT were not met within the proposed guidelines, and the automobile manufacturers were required to phase in either air bags or automatic belts (TRB 1989, 12).

12. This ruling has been vigorously opposed by highway safety groups, among others, who maintain that NHTSA could have examined other options such as stability standards for certain vehicle classes (Advocates for Highway and Auto Safety 1994).

13. However, because of the slow turnover of the vehicle fleet, it may be a decade or more before all vehicles on the road meet current regulatory requirements.

14. U.S. motor vehicle safety regulations, while extensive, do not include any field-of-view requirements, which are mandated in many European countries.

15. Estimates of crashes provided by the National Safety Council—11,200,000 motor vehicle crashes in 1994—were used for this calculation (Fearn et al. 1995, 78). Police-reported crashes, estimated at 6,492,000, are considerably lower (NHTSA 1995, i).

16. The primary source for the fatality and vehicle miles traveled figures is NHTSA (1995, i).

17. The automatic protection requirement of FMVSS 208, which affected model years 1987 and later, also contributed to reductions in fatality risk (Kahane et al. 1994, 13).

18. In 1989 there were 0.95 vehicles per person of driving age (Lave 1992, 5–7), indicating that nearly all of those eligible to drive have access to a car.

## REFERENCES

### Abbreviations

| | |
|---|---|
| AAMA | American Automobile Manufacturers Association |
| FHWA | Federal Highway Administration |
| GAO | General Accounting Office |
| IIHS | Insurance Institute for Highway Safety |

NHTSA     National Highway Traffic Safety Administration
TRB       Transportation Research Board

AAMA. 1994. Response to Docket No. 91-68, Notice 3, No. 47. *Comments on Consumer Information Regulations; Rollover Prevention*. Detroit, Mich., Oct. 20, 71 pp.

Advocates for Highway and Auto Safety. 1994. Response to Docket No. 91-68, Notice 3, No. 35. *Petition for Reconsideration: Termination of Rulemaking on Light Passenger Vehicle Rollover Prevention*. Washington, D.C., Aug. 30, 55 pp.

Booz, Allen Applied Research. 1976. *Final Phase I Report, The Automobile Consumer Information Study, Title II, P.L. 92-513*. DOT-HS-803-254. Bethesda, Md., June, 184 pp.

Crandall, R.W., H.K. Gruenspecht, T.E. Keeler, and L.B. Lave. 1986. *Regulating the Automobile*. The Brookings Institution, Washington, D.C., 202 pp.

Evans, L. 1991. *Traffic Safety and the Driver*. Van Nostrand Reinhold, New York, 405 pp.

Evans, L. 1994. Small Cars, Big Cars: What Is the Safety Difference? *Chance*, Vol. 7, No. 3, pp. 9–16.

Fearn, K.T., L. Kao, and T. Miller. 1995. *Accident Facts, 1995 Edition*. National Safety Council, Itasca, Ill.

*Federal Register*. 1994. Consumer Information Regulations; Federal Motor Vehicle Safety Standards; Rollover Prevention. NHTSA, U.S. Department of Transportation. Vol. 59, No. 123, June 28, pp. 33,254–33,272.

GAO. 1994. *Highway Safety: Factors Affecting Involvement in Vehicle Crashes*. GAO/PEMD-95-3. Washington, D.C., Oct., 46 pp.

Gillespie, T.D. 1992. *Fundamentals of Vehicle Dynamics*. Society of Automotive Engineers, Inc., Warrendale, Pa.

Graham, J.D. 1989. *Auto Safety: Assessing America's Performance*. Auburn House Publishing Co., Dover, Mass.

IIHS. 1994a. Response to Docket No. 91-68, Notice 3, No. 54. *Consumer Information Regulations; Federal Motor Vehicle Safety Standards; Rollover Prevention*. Arlington, Va., Oct. 21, 4 pp.

IIHS. 1994b. *Shopping for a Safer Car*. Arlington, Va., Sept.

IIHS. 1994c. Special Issue: Driver Death Rates by Vehicle Make and Series. *Status Report*, Vol. 29, No. 11, Oct. 8.

Kahane, C.J., J.R. Hackney, and A.M. Berkowitz. 1994. *Correlation of Vehicle Performance in the New Car Assessment Program with Fatality Risk in Actual Head-On Collisions*. No. 94-S8-O-ll. National Highway Traffic Safety Administration, 17 pp.

Lave, C. 1992. Cars and Demographics. *Access*, No. 1, Fall, pp. 4–11.

Magat, W.A., and W.K. Viscusi. 1992. *Informational Approaches to Regulation*. MIT Press, Cambridge, Mass.

S.W. Morris & Co. 1993. *Focus Groups on Traffic Safety Issues: Public Response to NCAP*. DTNH22-90-C-07015. Bethesda, Md., Aug. 23, 51 pp.

NHTSA and FHWA. 1991. *Moving America More Safely*. U.S. Department of Transportation, Sept., 61 pp.

NHTSA. 1993. *New Car Assessment Program*. Response to the NCAP FY 1992 Congressional Requirements. U.S. Department of Transportation, Dec., 125 pp.

NHTSA. 1995. *Traffic Safety Facts 1994*. DOT-HS-808-292. U.S. Department of Transportation, Aug.

O'Neill, B. 1995. *The Physics of Car Crashes and the Role of Vehicle Size and Weight in Occupant Protection*. IIHS, July, 14 pp.

Perchonok, K. 1972. *Accident Cause Analysis*. Cornell Aeronautical Laboratory, Inc., Ithaca, N.Y., July.

Sabey, B. 1973. *Accident Analysis in Great Britain*. Transport and Road Research Laboratory, Crowthorne, Berkshire, United Kingdom, Oct.

Svenson, O. 1981. Are We All Less Risky and More Skillful Than Our Fellow Drivers? *Acta Psychologica*, No. 47, pp. 143–148.

Treat, J.R., et al. 1979. *Tri-Level Study of the Causes of Traffic Accidents 1979*. DOT HS-034-3-545. Indiana University, Bloomington.

TRB. 1989. *Special Report 224: Safety Belts, Airbags, and Child Restraints*. National Research Council, Washington, D.C., 69 pp.

TRB. 1990. *Special Report 229: Safety Research for a Changing Highway Environment*. National Research Council, Washington, D.C., 166 pp.

TRB. 1991. *Special Report 232: Advanced Vehicle and Highway Technologies*. National Research Council, Washington, D.C., 90 pp.

U.S. Congress. House of Representatives. 1972. House Report No. 92-1033. April 28.

U.S. Congress. Senate. 1971. Senate Report No. 92-413. Oct. 28.

Williams, A.F., N.N. Paek, and A.K. Lund. 1995. Factors That Drivers Say Motivate Safe Driving Practices. *Journal of Safety Research*, Vol. 26, No. 2, pp. 119–124.

# 2

---

## CURRENT UNDERSTANDING OF MOTOR VEHICLE CRASH AVOIDANCE AND CRASHWORTHINESS

The characteristics and features of a motor vehicle that affect its safety can be classified into two broad categories: those helping the driver avoid a crash (crash avoidance) and those helping to protect vehicle occupants from harm during a crash (crashworthiness). Both aspects of vehicle safety are appropriate candidates for consumer information. In this chapter, the primary sources of information about vehicle-related factors affecting crash avoidance and crashworthiness are identified and the current state of knowledge about each is summarized. In the final section, a critical appraisal of the strengths and weaknesses of current knowledge is provided as a basis for developing meaningful consumer information about vehicle safety.

### VEHICLE SAFETY DATA

The primary types of data available to analyze vehicle crash avoidance potential and vehicle crashworthiness are (*a*) engineering data and (*b*) crash data. The former, which include crash tests, are supported by research on injury mechanisms and human tolerance to impacts.

### Engineering Data

Engineering data are physical measurements taken under static or dynamic conditions to predict vehicle crash avoidance potential and vehicle crashworthiness. Engineering data based on crash tests that measure vehicle crashworthiness are the most advanced. The National Highway Traffic Safety Administration (NHTSA) has more than 15 years of experience with the New Car Assessment Program (NCAP), whose primary purpose is to provide consumers with information on the relative crashworthiness of passenger vehicles as measured in full-frontal crash tests. The tests are conducted at 56 km/hr (35 mph)—8 km/hr (5 mph) more and with 35 percent greater energy than the federal certification standard, Federal Motor Vehicle Safety Standard (FMVSS) 208, so that differences in frontal crashworthiness performance among vehicles can be more readily observed (NHTSA 1993, 2–4). NHTSA has also developed a dynamic crash test to measure vehicle crashworthiness in side-impact crashes in which the vehicle is struck in the side by a barrier traveling at 54.6 km/hr (33.5 mph) (DOT 1994). Agency requests to expand the NCAP to include side-impact crash testing, however, have not been funded. The Insurance Institute for Highway Safety (IIHS), a nonprofit scientific and educational organization supported by the insurance industry, has recently begun testing vehicle crashworthiness in frontal offset crashes.[1] However, there is no federal safety standard relating to offset frontal crashes, and NHTSA does not conduct offset frontal crash tests itself.

Very few engineering data are available on how vehicle characteristics affect the potential for a vehicle to be involved in a crash. As part of its recent rulemaking on rollover prevention (*Federal Register* 1994), NHTSA proposed two vehicle stability metrics,[2] which agency analyses had shown to be significant predictors of vehicle propensity to roll over. The automobile industry, however, challenged NHTSA's finding that the stability metrics explain about half of the variability in rollover likelihood in single-vehicle accidents for the population of passenger vehicles and light trucks examined (*Federal Register* 1994, 33,260). Industry analysts maintained that the role of the vehicle, as measured by the stability metrics, is overstated relative to the role of environmental and driver factors in rollover crashes, and that vehicles with the same static stability measures have widely varying rollover crash experience (AAMA 1994, 1).[3]

Consumers Union, which publishes the popular *Consumer Reports*, has developed a simple dynamic test, which it believes better represents real-world emergency handling and vehicle rollover propensity. The test measures vehicle stability and handling in a double lane change maneuver typical of ordinary driving. Vehicles are driven at increasing speeds up to the point at which the vehicle is no longer controllable.

## Biomechanics Research

Research in biomechanics (the study of injury mechanisms and human tolerances to trauma) provides the basic knowledge to support the development of testing devices and, from these, performance standards for testing vehicle crashworthiness.[4] To understand how injuries are sustained and how to prevent or minimize the severity of such injuries in crashes, biomechanical engineers examine the mechanism of a particular injury associated with a given type of impact and how a body region responds to that impact. Impact tests are typically performed on cadavers in laboratories equipped with impact sleds and pendulum-type impactors.

Once the injury mechanism is understood, the next step is to determine how much of an impact a given body region can withstand before it becomes severely injured, that is, to establish a threshold of human tolerance. This threshold is typically set at a moderate level of injury for a given impact severity, because it would be too expensive to manufacture cars that allow the average occupant to walk away uninjured from a severe crash. Having determined these two crucial components of injury biomechanics—the injury mechanism and the human tolerance level—crashworthiness performance standards can be established. However, consumers should be made aware that there is a wide variation in human tolerance, which is primarily a function of age and gender. For example, many postmenopausal females suffer from osteoporosis, or bone loss, and may be injured in a crash from which a 20-year-old male can walk away.

Testing occupant protection in controlled crash situations has also necessitated development of anthropomorphic test dummies, better known as crash dummies. The data to build the dummies were developed from the human response studies using cadavers. The goal was to make the dummies respond in as human a fashion as possible. Different dummies have been developed for different crash configurations (e.g., frontal impact, side impact) and for different ages, heights, and weights. Crash tests for certification and consumer information purposes are based on 50th percentile males, that is, a 5-ft 8-in. male weighing 170 lb (Wolkomir 1995, 31).

## Crash Data

NHTSA, the states, and the insurance industry have developed data bases that provide information on the incidence and outcome of highway crashes. NHTSA has developed the primary traffic accident data bases. The oldest is the Fatal Accident Reporting System (FARS), which has provided an annual census of fatal traffic crashes since 1975 (NHTSA 1994, 3).

A companion data base to provide information on nonfatal crashes, the National Accident Sampling System (NASS), has been in operation since 1979. To reduce costs and tailor the system to meet user needs, NASS was recently restructured into two data collection systems: (a) a General Estimates System to provide national estimates of crashes by type from police accident reports without intensive follow-up crash investigations and (b) a Crashworthiness Data System (CDS) based on detailed information of a small sample of crashes to support research directly related to injury and crashworthiness of passenger cars and light truck vehicles. Other specialized data files, such as the Crash Avoidance Research Data File, have been developed to provide information for examining the relationships between vehicle design characteristics and crash likelihood in support of crash avoidance research.

Most states have computerized accident data systems based on police accident reports, which include information on fatal and injury crashes. Criteria for reporting property-damage only accidents, however, vary from state to state, as do the overall consistency and level of detail of the information.

The Highway Loss Data Institute (HLDI) is closely associated with IIHS. Both are funded by the automobile insurance industry. HLDI collects claims information from the major insurance companies and summarizes injury, collision, and theft losses of passenger cars and light truck vehicles. Injury losses are presented as the frequency of insurance claims made under personal injury protection insurance coverage in "no-fault" states (HLDI 1994).[5] The use of no-fault states helps ensure that the claims associated with a vehicle are for the occupants of that vehicle only—under no-fault each covered vehicle is responsible for its own occupants regardless of "fault" in the collision. However, information is not included on the costs of injuries paid either from personal health insurance coverage or bodily injury liability from other vehicles (Council et al. 1995, 10), or on the actual injury or severity of the injury that occurred.

## Data Issues

Each of the data sources just discussed has strengths and limitations as a basis for providing consumer safety information. Consumers are interested in the safety of motor vehicles as they are operated in the real world. Crash data for specific makes and models of vehicles can provide this type of information. However, real-world crashes are the product of many factors. Thus, isolating vehicle-related factors from the other factors, particularly human error and environmental conditions that affect crash likelihood and severity, is difficult. In addition, crash data are retrospective; the on-road crash performance of a particular car can only be evaluated after a few years' experience on the highway, leaving an information gap for purchasers of new car models. Finally, existing crash data bases are themselves limited by reliability issues and by differences in reporting criteria, variable definitions across reporting jurisdictions, and availability of critical variables of interest.

Crash tests offer a controlled setting that can help isolate the vehicle-related variables of interest. Here, too, reliability issues are a concern. Repeated measurements under the same conditions using the same vehicle make and model should yield similar test results. In addition, the crash tests should be valid indicators of actual crash experience. As discussed subsequently, the reliability and validity of NHTSA's NCAP crash test results are an issue.

One alternative for improving the predictive power of crash tests is to combine the crash test results for specific vehicle makes and models with occupant injury experience in prior crashes involving similar (i.e., "clone") vehicles. The idea is that at least some of the nonvehicle factors affecting crash outcomes could be controlled by introducing real-world data for vehicles similar to the crash-tested vehicle. A recent study of the feasibility of this approach (Council et al. 1995) found that the addition of crash injury data did improve the ability to predict future crash experience of new cars. The head injury measurements from the crash test, the medical claims data for predecessor vehicles from HLDI, and the proportion of severe driver injury in crashes involving predecessor vehicles were statistically significant predictors of expected injury for the new vehicle. However, the overall predictive ability of the model was not high, reflecting the continuing difficulty of controlling for the nonvehicle factors that affect crash outcomes (Council et al. 1995, 17–19).[6] In the absence of information about clones, the addition of information about vehicle weight and size—key variables affecting crashworthiness—should further improve the predictive capability of the model.[7]

## CURRENT STATE OF KNOWLEDGE FROM AVAILABLE DATA

Vehicle characteristics and safety features affect the likelihood of being in a crash as well as the crashworthiness of the vehicle once a crash has occurred. However, the relationship between vehicle characteristics and crash likelihood is not as well understood.

## Crash Avoidance

Crash avoidance research has traditionally taken a secondary role in NHTSA's motor vehicle safety research program, in part because of the difficulty of isolating the contribution of vehicle characteristics to crash potential (TRB 1990, 145). The probability of being in a crash is somewhat related to vehicle design components, such as rollover propensity, steering sensitivity, and braking performance, but it is perhaps most related to the characteristics and behavior of the driver (Council et al. 1995, 2).

Nevertheless, NHTSA has conducted research on vehicle-related measures to reduce the likelihood of crash involvement. Avoidance of rollover crashes has been a priority of NHTSA's crash avoidance research program (TRB 1990, 145). The popularity of sport utility vehicles and the evidence that their rollover propensity is higher than that of some passenger vehicles put pressure on the agency to develop a vehicle stability standard in the late 1980s. Two petitions, one from Congressman Wirth in 1986 and the other from Consumers Union in 1988, provided the basis for initiation of a formal agency rulemaking process in 1992 (NHTSA 1992, 5–6).[8] The agency proposed two static vehicle stability metrics, described earlier in this chapter, for a possible vehicle standard. Because of sharp differences of opinion over whether these measures are accurate predictors of real-world rollover crashes and cost-effectiveness considerations,[9] NHTSA decided to terminate regulation of a vehicle rollover standard (*Federal Register* 1994, 33,258).[10] Research and rulemaking are continuing, however, on such vehicle-related rollover crash avoidance features as antilock brakes[11] and on provision of consumer information on vehicle rollover propensity.

Other than research on avoidance of rollover crashes, the primary focus in NHTSA's crash avoidance research program has been on technology improvements—brake lighting, better tire and brake performance, and vehicle conspicuity. Studies of the effectiveness of many of these technology improvements have indicated only modest differences in crash likelihood. For example, antilock brakes have not provided as large a safety benefit as predicted.[12] One reason may be the small number of circumstances in which antilock brakes can help; fewer crashes involve loss of control that could be prevented with antilock brakes than were supposed (IIHS 1995a, 4, 5). Another explanation may lie in improper use of the brakes. Some consumers apparently continue to pump the brakes.[13]

New vehicle technologies that may have greater potential for assisting the driver in avoiding crashes are being developed in conjunction with the Intelligent Transportation Systems (ITS) program. Such new technologies as enhanced night vision and collision avoidance systems could significantly improve the type of information given to drivers and the speed with which it is provided. Thus, although the driver-vehicle interaction in crash avoidance is still not well understood, crash avoidance technologies may yield significant payoffs as ITS safety-related vehicle technology improvements are introduced.

## Crashworthiness

Driver and other vehicle occupant characteristics, such as age, belt use, and position at the time of a crash, affect injury outcome. Design features, such as vehicle size and weight and occupant compartment integrity, also play a dominant role in determining vehicle crashworthiness and occupant protection. Thus, NHTSA's motor vehicle safety research program has given top priority to research on measures to improve vehicle crashworthiness (TRB 1990, 41).

Crash data provide a good indication of the key vehicle-related factors that affect crash outcomes as well as the types of crashes that lead to most of the deaths and injuries on the nation's highways.

### Vehicle Size and Weight

Vehicle size and weight are consistent predictors of injury likelihood in all types of crashes. All else being equal, big and heavy cars offer more protection to their occupants than small and light cars (O'Neill 1995, 1). Although there is some question whether car size or car mass is the more important feature (Evans 1994; Evans and Frick 1992; O'Neill 1995), in practice there is a close relationship between the two. Typically, a large car is heavy, and a small car is light (Evans 1994, 14).

The effect of weight or mass is large. On the basis of a relationship derived from FARS data on more than 40,000 driver fatalities (Evans and Frick 1993, 215), when two cars whose masses differ by a factor of 2 crash into each other, the driver of the lighter car is 12 times as likely to be killed as the driver of the heavier car (Figure 2-1). However, the weight differential between cars involved in most multiple-vehicle crashes typically is smaller,[14] and when single-vehicle crashes are taken into account,[15] the probability of fatality averaged over all crash types is 2 to 3 times greater for the driver of a lighter car than for a driver of a heavier car (Evans 1989, 1,152). Furthermore, larger cars are more likely to have additional crush space to protect the integrity of the occupant compartment in more severe crashes.

Crash data indicate that the importance of vehicle weight and size holds across vehicle types. Occupants of small vehicles—whether cars, pickup trucks, or sport utility vehicles—are at much greater risk of fatal injury (all else being equal) taking into account the numbers of these vehicles on the road (Figure 2-2). Fatality rates are 1.5 to 2.5 times higher for occupants of the smallest vehicles than for occupants of the largest vehicles in each vehicle class (Figure 2-2).[16]

Despite the effect of vehicle weight and size on injury likelihood, the purchase of larger and heavier cars is not necessarily the best outcome from society's perspective. For example, occupants of a heavier car crashing with a lighter car are better protected, but at the expense of the occupants of the lighter car (O'Neill 1995, 5). Even if all car drivers choose to drive vehicles of the same mass, the range of other vehicles on the road—from bicycles to heavy trucks—is such that differences in mass could not be controlled (Evans 1994, 15). Moreover, mass is not a major factor in single-vehicle crashes, which account for 58 percent of all fatal crashes (NHTSA 1994, 43). In particular, vehicle size (i.e., vehicle length and track width) is the key factor in rollover crashes, which are a predominantly single-vehicle crash type (Evans 1994, 13). Finally, there are trade-offs between vehicle size and weight and other factors, such as fuel economy; smaller and lighter cars are more fuel efficient (Evans 1994, 16; Lave 1981). Consumers should be given information about the effect of vehicle size and weight on injury likelihood, but this is only one factor that must be considered in vehicle purchase decisions.

## Crash Types

Crash data can also help identify crash types that lead to most of the deaths and injuries on the nation's highways. Data available from NHTSA's CDS[17] indicate that vehicles involved in frontal crashes ac-

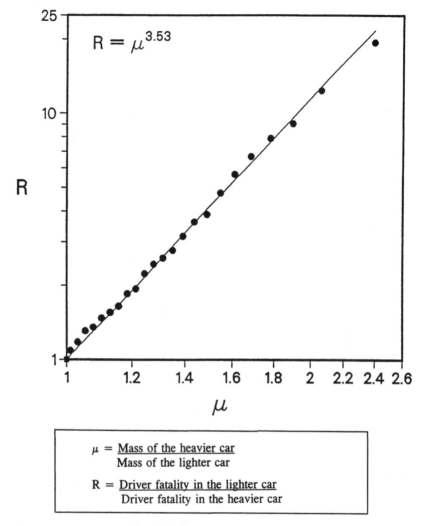

FIGURE 2-1   The ratio, R, of driver fatalities in the lighter car to driver fatalities in the heavier car versus the ratio, $\mu$, of the mass of the heavier car to the mass of the lighter car for frontal crashes, 1975–1989 FARS data. Modified and reprinted from *Accident Analysis and Prevention,* Vol. 25, No. 2, L. Evans and M.C. Frick, Mass Ratio and Relative Driver Fatality Risk in Two-Vehicle Crashes, pp. 213–224, copyright 1993, with kind permission from Elsevier Science Ltd., The Boulevard, Langford Lane, Kidlington 0X5 1GB, United Kingdom.

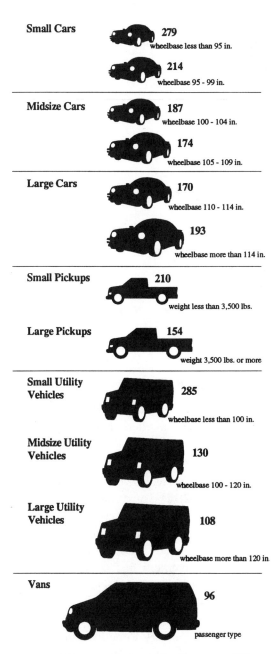

**Small Cars**

279
wheelbase less than 95 in.

214
wheelbase 95 - 99 in.

**Midsize Cars**

187
wheelbase 100 - 104 in.

174
wheelbase 105 - 109 in.

**Large Cars**

170
wheelbase 110 - 114 in.

193
wheelbase more than 114 in.

**Small Pickups**

210
weight less than 3,500 lbs.

**Large Pickups**

154
weight 3,500 lbs. or more

**Small Utility Vehicles**

285
wheelbase less than 100 in.

**Midsize Utility Vehicles**

130
wheelbase 100 - 120 in.

**Large Utility Vehicles**

108
wheelbase more than 120 in.

**Vans**

96
passenger type

FIGURE 2-2  Occupant deaths per million registered vehicles, 1990–1993 average (data compiled by Highway Loss Data Institute from FARS and R.L. Polk's National Vehicle Population Profile).

PERCENT VEHICLE INVOLVEMENT IN
FATAL AND INJURY CRASHES

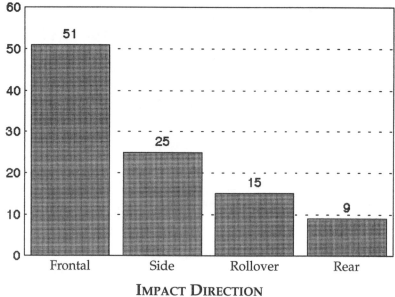

IMPACT DIRECTION

**FIGURE 2-3 Incidence of vehicle involvement in crashes by crash type and severity, 1990–1993 average (data compiled by NHTSA from NASS-CDS file).**

count for 51 percent of vehicles involved in crashes that result in fatalities and injuries (Figure 2-3). The next most common crash types from the standpoint of vehicle involvement are side-impact crashes, rollovers, and rear-impact crashes, which account for 25, 15, and 9 percent, respectively, of all vehicles involved in fatal and injury crashes (Figure 2-3). Vehicle involvement in frontal-, side-, and rear-impact crashes occurs primarily in multiple-vehicle collisions, whereas vehicle involvement in rollovers is more common in single-vehicle crashes.

When the data are disaggregated by vehicle type, it appears that vehicles differ in their propensity to be involved in various types of crashes (Figure 2-4). The largest difference is for vehicles involved in rollover crashes. Light truck vehicles—sport utility vehicles, pickups, and vans—are more than twice as likely as passenger cars to be involved in rollover crashes involving fatalities and injuries (Figure 2-4). However, light truck vehicles are somewhat less likely to be involved in side-impact crashes.

## Percent Vehicle Involvement in Fatal and Injury Crashes

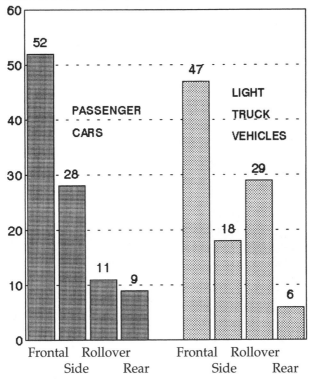

IMPACT DIRECTION

**FIGURE 2-4   Incidence of vehicle involvement in crashes by crash type, severity, and vehicle type, 1990–1993 average (data compiled by NHTSA from NASS-CDS file).**

The outcomes of crashes—the extent to which they involve vehicle occupant fatalities and injuries—are also a good indicator of the most serious crash types (Figure 2-5). Vehicles involved in rollover crashes have the largest share of vehicle occupant fatalities relative to the occurrence of vehicle involvement in this type of crash, and vehicles involved in side-impact crashes have the next largest share. For example, vehicles involved in rollover crashes represent 15 percent of vehicles involved in all fatal and injury crashes (Figure 2-3), but one-third of vehicle occupant fatalities occur in these crashes (Figure 2-5). Similarly,

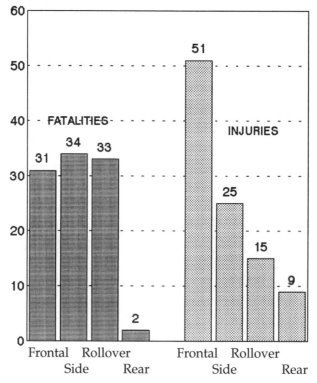

**FIGURE 2-5   Outcome of crashes by crash type and severity level, 1990–1993 average (data compiled by NHTSA from NASS-CDS file).**

vehicles involved in side-impact crashes represent slightly more than one-quarter of vehicles involved in all fatal and injury crashes, but they account for slightly more than one-third of vehicle occupant fatalities. Vehicles involved in frontal crashes account for the largest share of vehicle occupant injuries, almost twice the share of the next largest injury source—vehicles involved in side-impact crashes (Figure 2-5).

**Frontal Crashes**  Frontal crashes typically involve more than one vehicle. Vehicle involvement in such crashes accounts for the largest share of fatalities and injuries of all crash types (Figure 2-6). (The data for

## INCIDENCE OF VEHICLE INVOLVEMENT IN FATAL AND INJURY FRONTAL CRASHES

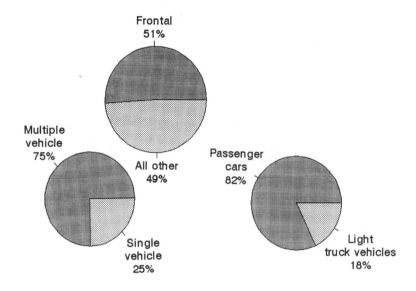

## FATALITY OUTCOMES OF VEHICLES INVOLVED IN FRONTAL CRASHES

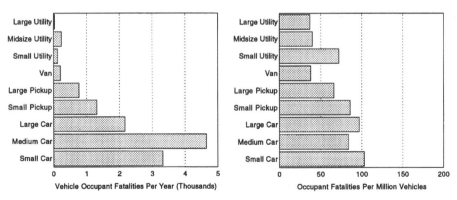

FIGURE 2-6   Frontal crash statistics, 1990–1993 average (data on vehicle involvement in crashes compiled by NHTSA from NASS-CDS file; data on fatality outcomes compiled by Highway Loss Data Institute from FARS and R.L. Polk's National Vehicle Population Profile).

the pie charts in Figures 2-6, 2-8, 2-9, and 2-10 are given in Table 2-1.) Most fatalities are represented by occupants of passenger cars, but fatality rates are more evenly distributed when measured by vehicle type (Figure 2-6).[18]

Because of the severity of frontal crashes, top priority has been given to research on measures to improve vehicle crashworthiness in frontal crashes (TRB 1990, 41). Substantial resources have gone into the study of injuries sustained by occupants in frontal crashes and the development of the Hybrid III crash dummy to test the injury reduction potential of occupant protection devices, such as seat belt systems and air bags. After several years, this research resulted in establishment of injury tolerance levels and performance standards based on acceleration measured at the head and chest and loads measured on the upper legs of crash dummies in frontal crash tests (TRB 1990, 144).[19] FMVSS 208 requires that new automobiles not exceed injury thresholds measured in a 48-km/hr (30-mph) full-frontal barrier crash test using instrumented, safety-belted dummies in the driver and passenger seats. The companion NCAP has provided consumer information since 1979 on vehicle performance in full-frontal crashes for a more demanding 56-km/hr (35-mph) test.[20]

One problem with current frontal crash tests is their inadequate representation of real-world crash configurations. By definition, the crash tests measure the performance of vehicles of approximately the same weight, although real-world frontal crashes typically involve vehicles of various weights and sizes. The reason, according to NHTSA, is that the agency recognizes that consumers will continue to demand, and manufacturers will continue to produce, passenger vehicles of various weights and sizes. NHTSA's objective is to encourage manufactur-

TABLE 2-1 VEHICLE INVOLVEMENT IN FATAL AND INJURY CRASHES BY IMPACT DIRECTION, CRASH TYPE, AND VEHICLE TYPE, 1990–1993 AVERAGE (NHTSA, NASS-CDS FILE)

| | | CRASH TYPE | | VEHICLE TYPE | |
|---|---|---|---|---|---|
| IMPACT DIRECTION | TOTAL | MULTIPLE VEHICLE | SINGLE VEHICLE | PASSENGER CARS | LIGHT TRUCK VEHICLES |
| Frontal | 583,604 | 439,897 | 143,707 | 478,651 | 104,953 |
| Side | 290,793 | 244,927 | 45,866 | 250,582 | 40,211 |
| Rollover | 166,664 | 30,685 | 135,979 | 100,726 | 65,938 |
| Rear | 97,309 | 94,599 | 2,710 | 84,408 | 12,901 |

ers to provide the highest level of safety they can within each size class (personal communication, James Hackney, Office of Market Incentives, NHTSA, Aug. 10, 1995).

Even if the weight issue is disregarded, the current tests required for compliance with FMVSS 208 and for consumer information represent only a small fraction of real-world frontal crashes.[21] Vehicle involvement in offset crashes, in which the front ends of the opposing vehicles do not fully engage but overlap by 40 to 60 percent, is far more common (Figure 2-7).[22] In offset crashes, a smaller part of the car's structure must bear the crash energy, thus making intrusion into the occupant compartment more likely and increasing the potential for severe lower extremity injuries even for belted drivers in air bag–equipped cars (IIHS 1994, 6). In contrast to full-width frontal barrier tests that are most demanding of restraint systems, frontal offset crash tests are most demanding of the structural integrity of the occupant compartment (IIHS 1994, 1).

Progress is being made in understanding injuries in frontal offset crashes, particularly lower leg injuries, and developing appropriate test

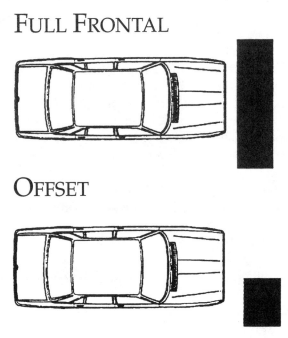

FIGURE 2-7   Comparison of full-frontal and frontal offset crash tests.

standards. For example, crash dummies are being modified so that lower extremity injuries can be studied. Standardized frontal tests that simulate offset frontal impacts are being developed. In 1995 IIHS conducted offset tests using deformable barriers[23] on 14 midsize cars. Australia conducts offset crash tests at a similar speed—64 km/hr (40 mph)—for its New Car Assessment Program. The European Union has announced that it will require vehicles to pass offset crash tests at 56 km/hr (35 mph)—8 km/hr (5 mph) less than the IIHS test speed but similar in other respects (IIHS 1995b, 5). To date, federal performance standards for impacts sustained in frontal offset crashes have not been established in the United States.

Crash test reliability is another issue that affects the use of frontal crash test results for consumer information. NCAP crash test results are based on testing only one vehicle of a particular make and model. An obvious question is whether the test results would be the same if the test were repeated. The most recent study of NCAP test variability was conducted in 1982 (Machey and Gauthier 1984) when NHTSA, in collaboration with the automobile industry, repeated 12 high-speed tests of a single vehicle model, the Chevrolet Citation, at three different testing facilities. Despite efforts to reduce variability, head injury criterion (HIC) values differed from test to test by a factor of 2 (from 500 to almost 1,000), chest loads by a factor of 1.3 (from 36 to 47), and femur loads by a factor of 3 (from 260 to 990) (presentation by Ernie Grush, Ford Motor Company, CASI Workshop, June 21, 1995). Unfortunately, because of the limited number of tests, it was not possible to quantify the sources of variability, which included the test procedure, test facilities, test instrumentation, test dummy used, and the individual vehicles (GAO 1995, 37).

Historical analyses of NCAP test results (Kahane et al. 1994, 3; GAO 1995, 30–36) have found both an absolute reduction (lower scores are better) and a convergence in overall test scores, although differences in test scores remain large.[24] NHTSA maintains that improvements have been made to reduce test variability, which is demonstrated by its analysis. In addition, passenger vehicles have become more uniform in their safety features, and crash dummies have become more sophisticated. However, there has not been an updated study to confirm the reductions in test variability.

A final issue with respect to frontal crash tests is how well they predict injury likelihood in real-world frontal crashes. A recent analysis conducted by NHTSA (Kahane et al. 1994) and presented to Congress

(Kahane 1994) found a statistically significant difference in fatality likelihood between belted drivers of cars that received good and poor scores as rated by NCAP either by a single injury criterion (e.g., head injury) or by a composite measure (e.g., a weighted combination of the scores for the three body regions).[25] In a head-on collision between cars of approximately equal mass, the belted driver of a good-scoring car has, on the average, about a 15 to 25 percent lower fatality risk than the driver of a poor-scoring car (Kahane 1994, xvii). However, there was no similar statistically significant difference between vehicles that rated exceptionally well and those that rated average on the NCAP test (Kahane 1994, xviii).

A recent analysis by the General Accounting Office (GAO) (1995) essentially confirmed NHTSA's findings. When vehicles were categorized by their NCAP scores, the bottom quintile with the worst NCAP scores had significantly higher fatality rates than the remaining 80 percent of the NCAP-tested vehicles (GAO 1995, 7–8). The results of both analyses suggest that the NCAP test results have some modest correlation with real-world crash performance.

In summary, knowledge about injuries sustained in frontal crashes is perhaps the most advanced of all crash types, and injury mitigation measures have been widely introduced. There is a history of more than 15 years with frontal crash tests and provision of consumer information about test results. Crash test results indicate a modest correlation with real-world crash performance. However, as crash test scores for new, air bag–equipped vehicle models converge in the future, it will become more difficult to distinguish valid differences in the frontal crashworthiness of vehicles.[26] In addition, reliability of information from current frontal crash tests is not well established.

**Side-Impact Crashes** Vehicles involved in side-impact crashes account for the second-largest share of fatalities and injuries of all crash types (Figure 2-8). As in frontal crashes, vehicles in side-impact crashes mostly comprise passenger vehicles in multiple-vehicle crashes (Figure 2-8). Fatality levels are high in these crashes, reflecting both the difficulty of protecting vehicle occupants in side-impact crashes and the overrepresentation of typically more vulnerable older drivers in this type of crash (TRB 1988, 49).

Because of the seriousness of side-impact crashes, the research emphasis during the mid-1970s shifted from mitigating injuries in frontal crashes to mitigating injuries in side-impact crashes (TRB

## INCIDENCE OF VEHICLE INVOLVEMENT IN FATAL AND INJURY SIDE-IMPACT CRASHES

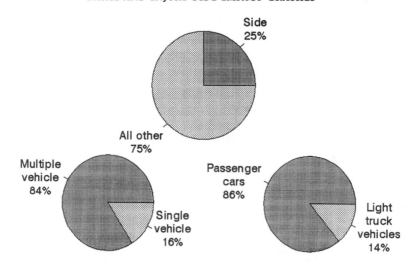

## FATALITY OUTCOMES OF VEHICLES INVOLVED IN SIDE IMPACT CRASHES

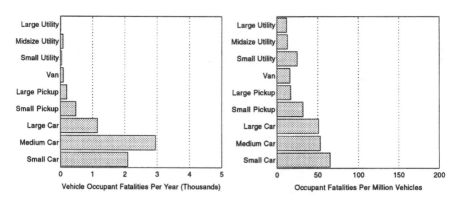

FIGURE 2-8   Side-impact crash statistics, 1990–1993 average (data on vehicle involvement in crashes compiled by NHTSA from NASS-CDS file; data on fatality outcomes compiled by Highway Loss Data Institute from FARS and R.L. Polk's National Vehicle Population Profile).

1990, 41). The research involved problem analysis and cadaver testing at various impact speeds. Results of the cadaver tests were used to relate crash impacts, measured by accelerations, to the probability of injury, which, in turn, was used to develop a side-impact dummy (SID) (TRB 1990, 144).

NHTSA first proposed a federal standard regarding tolerable levels of side impact in 1988. It has since been revised. FMVSS 214 now requires that passenger cars and light truck vehicles alike not exceed injury thresholds measured in a dynamic 54.6-km/hr (33.5-mph) crash test using a deformable barrier.[27] In response to the standard, manufacturers are protecting against side impact in current model vehicles by strengthening the side door, padding the inner door surfaces, and installing side-impact air bags (Haland 1994).

Despite an adequate understanding of the mechanisms of injury in side-impact crashes for crucial regions of the torso—the chest, abdomen, and pelvis—much work remains to be done. For example, the federal test criterion is still controversial and is not fully accepted by the biomechanical community, who have developed an alternative standard (Viano 1987).[28] The European community, which has recently approved side-impact crash testing for members of the European Union, will likely adopt the alternative injury standard and a competing crash dummy, known as EUROSID (IIHS 1995b, 5).

Although data on vehicle performance in side-impact crash tests are being collected, the ability of the test to forecast injury in real-world side-impact crashes that approximate the test has not been verified. Analyses similar to those prepared by NHTSA and GAO for frontal crash tests are needed.

Much work remains to be done to determine the most effective ways of preventing injury in side-impact crashes. This includes determining the best type of padding to use as well as the optimal pressure to be generated in a side-impact air bag.

For all these reasons, it is probably premature to provide consumers with information on the relative merits of side-impact safety features in current-model vehicles.

**Rollover Crashes** Vehicles involved in rollover crashes[29] account for about 15 percent of vehicles involved in all fatal and injury crashes. Like vehicles involved in side-impact crashes, they have a disproportionately high share of vehicle occupant fatalities relative to the occurrence of this crash type (Figures 2-3 and 2-5). However, rollover crashes exhibit many characteristics that distinguish them from other crash types (Figure 2-9). Rollover crashes are typically a single-vehicle phenomenon and involve a higher share of light truck vehicles than other crash types (Figure 2-9). Although most fatalities are occupants of passenger cars, utility vehicles and pickup trucks have the highest fatality rates (Figure 2-9).

The principal reason for severe and fatal injuries to occupants in vehicles involved in a rollover crash is ejection from the vehicle and the resulting head and neck injuries (Malliaris and Digges 1987; NHTSA 1992). These injuries can also be severe for unbelted occupants who are retained within the vehicle. According to NHTSA, ejections are responsible for nearly two-thirds of the fatalities, and safety belts are used by only 13 percent of fatally injured occupants (*Federal Register* 1994, 33,255). Belted occupants are least likely to sustain head and neck injuries but are not immune, particularly if roof crush occurs (Syson 1995).

Biomechanical engineers have measured the forces that result in severe neck injuries from an impact to the top of the head that can occur in a rollover crash (McElhaney and Myers 1993; Yoganandan et al. 1991). Because of the complexity of possible impacts and the range of occupant positions at the time of the crash, biomechanical solutions for the retained occupant are beyond the state of the art.[30]

Injury mitigation measures have concentrated on containing the occupant within the vehicle and softening impact blows. NHTSA's crashworthiness research is currently focused on such vehicle-related measures as sturdier door locks and latches, shatterproof side windows,[31] and increased roof strength (*Federal Register* 1994, 33,256). Testing devices have also been developed to help understand rollover crashes. For example, a rollover crash device that pitches vehicles over laterally after they first develop momentum by advancing down a track has been produced. The purpose is to understand better the tendency of different models to roll, once tripped, and the effect of roof crush on occupants during a rollover collision. Knowledge learned from these devices can also help improve simulations of vehicle rollover (TRB 1990, 144).

Because of the need for a better understanding of how injuries occur in rollover collisions, human tolerance levels and performance standards have not been established. Thus providing information to

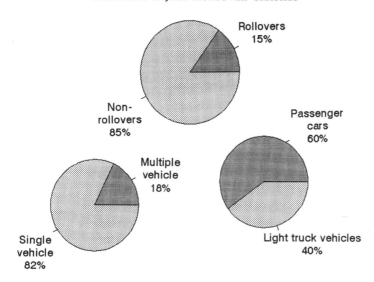

FATALITY OUTCOMES OF VEHICLES INVOLVED
IN ROLLOVER CRASHES

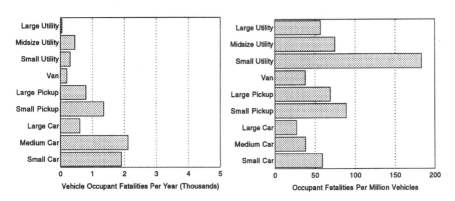

FIGURE 2-9   Rollover crash statistics, 1990–1993 average (data on vehicle involvement in crashes compiled by NHTSA from NASS-CDS file; data on fatality outcomes compiled by Highway Loss Data Institute from FARS and R.L. Polk's National Vehicle Population Profile).

consumers about the crashworthiness of passenger vehicles in rollover crashes is premature.

**Rear-Impact Crashes**  Vehicles involved in rear-impact crashes account for the smallest fraction (9 percent) of vehicles involved in all fatal and injury crashes among all crash types (Figure 2-10). This finding is not unexpected, because one of the most common crash types is a two-

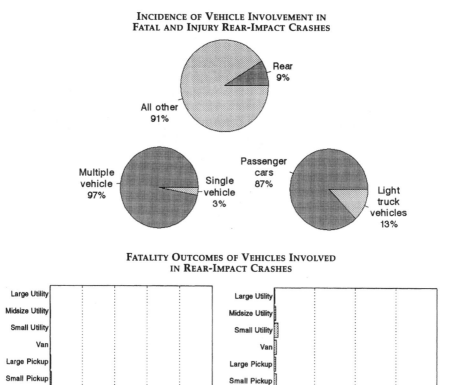

FIGURE 2-10  Rear-impact crash statistics, 1990–1993 average (data on vehicle involvement in crashes compiled by NHTSA from NASS-CDS file; data on fatality outcomes compiled by Highway Loss Data Institute from FARS and R.L. Polk's National Vehicle Population Profile).

vehicle fender bender, which does not result in life-threatening injuries. Rear-impact collisions predominantly involve passenger cars in multiple-vehicle crashes (Figure 2-10). Fatality levels are lower than in other crash types, and the rates are highest for passenger cars (Figure 2-10).[32]

The primary injury in rear-impact crashes is whiplash, but the mechanism of injury is not well understood.[33] Research is being done and some tests have been conducted.[34] There is evidence that head restraints reduce the probability of neck injury (Bourbeau et al. 1993; Kahane 1982; Ollson et al. 1990; Svenssan et al. 1993), and head restraints located behind and close to the back of the head are preferable. The level of knowledge is sufficient to provide consumers with information about head restraints but inadequate to provide general information about the crashworthiness of vehicles in rear-end collisions.

## Summary of the State of Knowledge

Since the federal role in regulating motor vehicle safety was established in 1966, major advances have been made in understanding injury mechanisms and human tolerance levels in crashes. The advances have provided the basis for vehicle safety performance standards and design improvements. The state of knowledge is most advanced in the area of vehicle crashworthiness, where the link between design features, such as vehicle size and weight and occupant compartment integrity, is strongly associated with how well the occupants are protected in a crash.

Vehicle weight and size are consistent predictors of injury likelihood in all types of crashes. The effect of vehicle weight or mass is large; the probability of a fatality, when averaged over all crash types, is 2 to 3 times greater for the driver of a lighter car than for the driver of a heavier car. Larger cars are more likely to have additional crush space to protect the integrity of the occupant compartment in more severe crashes.

Knowledge about frontal crashes, the most common of the crash types that result in death and injury, is the best developed. Injury mechanisms and human tolerances are well understood, performance standards have been established, and frontal crash tests for certification and consumer information purposes have been conducted for more than 15 years. However, important gaps in understanding remain. Full-frontal crash tests reflect only a small fraction of the real-world variation in crash speeds and configurations even for frontal crashes. Knowledge about potential variance in crash test scores is insufficient, which calls into question the repeatability of test results. Finally, these crash test results have a modest correlation with real-world crash performance. The correlation could be improved by combining crash test results with actual crash data. However, by their nature, crash tests are unlikely ever to have a high correlation with on-road crashes because they cannot reflect important driver and vehicle use characteristics.

Knowledge about side-impact crashes, another common crash type, is also well advanced. Injury mechanisms and human tolerances are adequately understood, and performance standards and test criteria have been established. However, the U.S. test standards are not fully accepted by the biomechanical community, and much work remains to be done before consumers can be provided valid data about injury protection in side-impact crashes.

Mechanisms for reducing injury when vehicles roll over are not well understood. Knowledge about injury in rear-impact crashes, which account for the smallest fraction of severe crashes, is also limited. Research is being conducted, but except for information on head restraints, the level of knowledge has not advanced to the stage that general information on the relative crashworthiness of vehicles in rollover or rear-end collisions can be made available to consumers.

How vehicle design features affect the likelihood of being in a crash is less well understood, reflecting in part the importance of other factors, particularly driver behavior, in crash causation. Research has focused on technology enhancements, such as improvements in braking systems and vehicle conspicuity, but most of these advances have made only modest differences in crash likelihood. New technologies that have the potential to provide great assistance to drivers and reduce crash likelihood significantly are being introduced as part of the ITS program, such as enhanced night driving and collision avoidance systems. Thus, the role of vehicle factors in avoiding crashes is an important area for continued research.

In summary, the current level of understanding about vehicle safety characteristics and features—both their effect on crash likelihood and the protection they afford to vehicle occupants—is not well enough advanced to provide consumers with a definitive assessment, based strictly on scientific grounds, of the highway safety performance of a new vehicle. By the same token, there is a good understanding of key vehicle-related factors that affect crash outcomes, such as vehicle size and weight, and of design features, such as energy absorption, that can reduce injury potential. There is also considerable experience with frontal crash test results that offer some modest correlation with real-world crash experience. With further work, plus expert judgment, this understanding can provide the foundation for giving consumers more predictive measures of the overall safety of new motor vehicles.

## NOTES

1. The 64-kph (40-mph) test speed, higher than the 56- to 60-kph (35- to 37.5-mph) speed being considered for the European standard, was selected for the same reason that the NCAP test is conducted at 8 kph (5 mph) above the compliance standards—high speeds magnify differences among cars.
2. The two metrics were critical sliding velocity and tilt table angle. Critical sliding velocity is a measure of the minimum lateral (sideways) vehicle velocity required to initiate rollover when the vehicle is tripped by something in the roadway (e.g., a curb). Tilt table angle is the angle at which the last uphill tire of the vehicle lifts off a platform as the platform is increasingly tilted (*Federal Register* 1994, 33,259).
3. The Transportation Analysis Institute, an independent company, has developed a rollover stability index—the K index, which is purported to have a good correlation with actual crash data. The index includes four factors—vehicle track width, vehicle height, vehicle weight, and vehicle weight above a certain height—but the specific calculations are proprietary (personal communication, Joseph Kimmel, Transportation Analysis Institute, July 13, 1995).
4. A more detailed description of research in impact biomechanics can be found elsewhere (NRC 1985; Viano et al. 1989).
5. Collision and theft losses are reported as average loss payments per insured vehicle year (i.e., the claim frequency times the average loss payment per claim) (HLDI 1994).
6. The researchers expected that, in such a multifactor situation, the variables that can be measured and be expected to remain constant for a given make and model, such as crash test variables and the clone vehicle crash and insurance information, would have a modest predictive ability. The results of the study support this hypothesis (Council et al. 1995, 18).
7. The model of Council et al. takes size and weight into account in that the crash-tested vehicle and its clones are approximately the same weight. Unlike crash-tested vehicles, the clone vehicles are involved in crashes with vehicles of different weights, representing different types of crashes (e.g., multiple-vehicle and single-vehicle crashes). Therefore, with this approach it is possible to predict crashworthiness across vehicles—a crash-tested vehicle and its clones will have one predicted injury outcome; a different vehicle and its clones will have another. Although not attempted in the study by

Council et al., information about vehicle weight and size could be substituted for the clone data if clones for a particular new make or model vehicle are not available.

8. Congressman Wirth's petition, which proposed a specific minimum static stability factor among other requests, was denied because the approach was considered too narrow and inappropriate (NHTSA 1992, 5–6). Consumers Union's petition, which recommended "a minimum stability standard to protect against unreasonable risk of rollover," was granted in September 1988 (NHTSA 1992, 6). NHTSA had issued an Advance Notice of Proposed Rulemaking on Rollover Resistance in 1973 to solicit comments on development of a test procedure, test conditions, and performance requirements to evaluate vehicle rollover propensities, but after reviewing comments to the docket and conducting several studies, the agency concluded the rulemaking until the factors contributing to rollover crashes could be better understood (NHTSA 1992, 5).

9. NHTSA analysis showed that setting a performance level high enough to affect passenger cars would require redesign of nearly all sport utility vehicles, vans, and pickup trucks. NHTSA concluded that the degree of redesign would have raised issues of public acceptance and possibly even the elimination of certain classes of vehicles as they are known today (*Federal Register* 1994, 33,258).

10. This ruling has been vigorously opposed by highway safety groups, among others, who maintain that NHTSA could have examined other options such as stability standards for certain vehicle classes (Advocates for Highway and Auto Safety 1994). NHTSA, however, found that its stability metrics, when applied to a specific class of vehicle rather than to all vehicles grouped together, lost much of their predictive power to explain rollover crash occurrence (*Federal Register* 1994, 33,258).

11. NHTSA published an advance notice of proposed rulemaking for antilock brake systems for light-duty vehicles, including cars, vans, pickup trucks, and sport utility vehicles on Jan. 4, 1994 (59 FR 281) (*Federal Register* 1994, 33,255).

12. Two studies by the Highway Loss Data Institute and one by NHTSA found that antilock brakes are not reducing the frequency or the cost of crashes as measured by insurance claims for vehicle damage (IIHS 1995a, 4, 5).

13. Yet another possibility is that drivers of vehicles with antilock brakes take more risks (e.g., drive faster on wet pavement than they would have), thus compensating for the risk reduction benefits of the new technology. This is an example of a phenomenon called risk compensation or risk homeostasis—the theory that drivers adjust their behavior in response to perceptions of the risks they face. Whether the phenomenon exists has been hotly debated and is the subject of a considerable literature (see Peltzman 1975; Wilde 1982; Graham 1982; Evans 1986; and Lund and O'Neill 1986).

14. Crashes with a 1.5 times mass ratio (i.e., one car is 50 percent heavier than the other) are more typical (personal communication, Leonard Evans, Gen-

eral Motors R&D Center, Dec. 20, 1995). In this case, the risk of fatality is greater by a factor of 4 for the driver of the lighter car involved in a crash with the 50 percent heavier car (Evans and Frick 1993, 214). The mass differential, however, may be growing as light truck vehicles become a larger share of the total passenger fleet. For example, data from FARS indicate that the fatality risk is 7 times greater for drivers of light cars involved in crashes with pickup trucks (Evans and Frick 1993, 222).

15. Fatality risk estimates are less certain for single-car crashes because of the difficulty of estimating exposure in single-car crashes.

16. One anomaly is the slight increase in fatality rates for the largest cars (i.e., wheelbase 114 in.). The explanation may be that very large cars are driven primarily by the old, who are more likely to die in a crash, thereby increasing the numerator of the fatality rate calculation. Of all the car classes, the largest car size has the smallest number of registered vehicles, thereby decreasing the denominator of the fatality rate calculation (personal communication, Maria Penny, Highway Loss Data Institute, Oct. 4, 1995).

17. CDS data are obtained from a nationally representative probability sample selected from all police-reported, tow-away crashes involving light-duty vehicles. For purposes of this analysis, crashes were included if they resulted in a fatality or an injury of any type, that is, ranging from a minor injury (Abbreviated Injury Scale 1) to a critical or maximum injury type (Abbreviated Injury Scale 5 or 6).

18. One anomaly is the fatality rate figure for medium-sized cars, which is lower than for large cars. One would have expected lower fatality rates for large cars because of their weight and size advantage.

19. Information was also developed on how injury criteria relate to injury risk. Biomechanical experts from Ford Motor Company and General Motors Corporation developed injury risk functions that relate the probability of injury risk to various acceleration levels for the head and chest injury criteria and for various load levels for the upper leg criterion (Hackney and Kahane 1995, 1–2).

20. Kinetic energy is proportional to the square of the velocity. Thus, there is 36 percent more kinetic energy in a 56-km/hr (35-mph) crash than in a 48-km/hr (30-mph) crash (NHTSA 1995).

21. On the basis of vehicle involvement in crashes gathered from the NASS-CDS for 1990 to 1993, only 1 percent of vehicles involved in frontal crashes resulting in fatalities and injuries are directly comparable with the fully frontal crash tests used for certification purposes and for the NCAP. Crashes are defined as fully frontal if they meet the following three criteria: (*a*) direction of force is at 12 o'clock; (*b*) crush profile is zero, that is, the centerline of the vehicle is directly aligned with the center of the direct damage; and (*c*) the crush damage on the left front of the vehicle is equivalent to the crush damage on the right front of the vehicle within 20 percent (criteria were defined by Carl Ragland, Office of Crashworthiness Research, NHTSA).

22. On the basis of the same NASS-CDS data for 1990 through 1993, 21 percent of vehicles involved in frontal crashes resulting in fatalities and injuries are classified as being in frontal offset crashes.

23. Deformable barriers were selected because they provide a reasonable approximation of how cars actually perform in offset crashes (IIHS 1994, 6).

24. For example, the HIC scores for vehicles in 1979 ranged from 521 to 4,513; in 1993 that range was between 273 and 1,459 (GAO 1995, 31).

25. By controlling for differences in driver age and sex as well as weight of the vehicle and examining only frontal crashes involving belted occupants, the researchers were able to isolate differences in vehicle crashworthiness.

26. It is conceivable that a combination of regulatory standards and voluntary efforts by the manufacturers could result in improvements in vehicle crashworthiness so large that, by the time a vehicle crashworthiness rating system is developed, the differences in crashworthiness between vehicles of equivalent weight would be less than could be predicted with statistical confidence by the rating. Should this occur, however, the process of developing the rating would have accomplished one of the primary objectives of a program to improve consumer vehicle safety information, that is, to provide additional incentives for the automobile manufacturers to enhance vehicle safety.

27. The vehicles are actually struck in the side by a barrier traveling at this speed (DOT 1994).

28. The federal standard uses the thoracic trauma index (TTI), which is based on the measured lateral accelerations on the spine and near-side rib of the SID. The industry maintained that TTI is not a good predictor of soft organ damage or overall injury probability in side-impact crashes. General Motors, in particular, developed an alternative criterion, known as the viscous criterion, which measures the extent of chest deflection and the speed of the chest wall, as well as a more humanlike dummy for side-impact testing, known as BIOSID. (BIOSID has a more flexible rib cage than SID.)

29. Crashes are defined here as rollover crashes if a vehicle rollover occurred either as the first harmful event or as a subsequent event (e.g., from a collision with another vehicle or object). This definition of rollover is used by NHTSA (NHTSA 1994, 185).

30. The forces causing severe neck injuries vary over a wide range depending on the extent of neck flexion or extension and on the configuration of the neck at the time of impact.

31. The effect of the use of shatterproof glass in side windows on head injuries in side-impact crashes must also be studied.

32. The scale for the fatality figures is the same as for the other crash impact directions—frontal, side, and rollover—to facilitate comparison.

33. One hypothesis of the injury mechanism is that the sudden forward acceleration of the struck vehicle causes a shearing effect to be developed between adjacent cervical vertebrae; this relative motion causes injury to the soft tissues connecting these vertebrae. Testing of this hypothesis is under

way (personal communication, Albert King, Wayne State University Bio-engineering Center, Sept. 6, 1995).

34. IIHS recently tested 164 head restraints for their ability to prevent whiplash (IIHS 1995c). Test results, however, have not yet been correlated with on-road crash injury rates.

# REFERENCES

## Abbreviations

| | |
|---|---|
| AAMA | American Automobile Manufacturers Association |
| DOT | U.S. Department of Transportation |
| GAO | General Accounting Office |
| HLDI | Highway Loss Data Institute |
| IIHS | Insurance Institute for Highway Safety |
| NHTSA | National Highway Traffic Safety Administration |
| NRC | National Research Council |
| TRB | Transportation Research Board |

AAMA. 1994. Response to Docket No. 91-68, Notice 3, No. 47. Comments on Consumer Information Regulations; Rollover Prevention. Detroit, Mich., Oct. 20, 71 pp.

Advocates for Highway and Auto Safety. 1994. Response to Docket No. 91-68, Notice 3, No. 35. *Petition for Reconsideration: Termination of Rulemaking on Light Passenger Vehicle Rollover Prevention.* Washington, D.C., Aug. 30, 55 pp.

Bourbeau, R., D. Desjardins, M. Maag, and C. Laberge-Nadeau. 1993. Neck Injuries Among Belted and Unbelted Occupants of the Front Seat of Cars. *Journal of Trauma,* Vol. 35, pp. 794–799.

Council, F.M., J.R. Stewart, and C.L. Cox. 1995. *Predicting Future Crashworthiness for New Cars: Exploration of a New Methodology.* University of North Carolina, Chapel Hill, July, 23 pp.

DOT. 1994. NHTSA Cites Safety Features in 1995 Cars, Trucks, and Vans. *News,* Office of the Assistant Secretary for Public Affairs, Washington, D.C., Oct. 6.

Evans, L. 1986. Risk Homeostasis Theory and Traffic Accident Data. *Risk Analysis,* Vol. 6, pp. 81–94.

Evans, L. 1989. Passive Compared to Active Approaches To Reducing Occupant Fatalities. *Proc., Twelfth International Technical Conference on Experimental Safety Vehicles,* Gothenburg, Sweden, May 29–June 1, NHTSA, U.S. Department of Transportation, Vol. 2, pp. 1,149–1,157.

Evans, L. 1994. Small Cars, Big Cars: What Is the Safety Difference? *Chance,* Vol. 7, No. 3., pp. 9–16.

Evans, L., and M.C. Frick. 1992. Car Size or Car Mass: Which Has Greater Influence on Fatality Risk? *American Journal of Public Health,* Vol. 82, No. 8, Aug., pp. 1,105–1,112.

Evans, L., and M.C. Frick. 1993. Mass Ratio and Relative Driver Fatality Risk in Two-Vehicle Crashes. *Accident Analysis and Prevention*, Vol. 25, No. 2, pp. 213–224.

*Federal Register*. 1994. Consumer Information Regulations; Federal Motor Vehicle Safety Standards; Rollover Prevention. NHTSA, U.S. Department of Transportation. Vol. 59, No. 123, June 28, pp. 33,254–33,272.

GAO. 1995. *Highway Safety: Reliability and Validity of DOT Crash Tests.* GAO/PEMD-95-5. May, 76 pp.

Graham, J.D. 1982. On Wilde's Theory of Risk Homeostasis. *Risk Analysis*, Vol. 2, pp. 235–237.

Hackney, J.R., and C.J. Kahane. 1995. The New Car Assessment Program: Five Star Rating System and Vehicle Safety Performance Characteristics. No. 950888. Presented at Society of Automotive Engineers International Congress and Exposition, Detroit, Mich., Feb. 27–Mar. 2, 16 pp.

Haland, Y. 1994. Background, Description, and Evaluation of a New Side Airbag System. *Proc., International Body Engineering Conference on Automotive Body Design and Engineering*, Detroit, Mich., pp. 74–80.

HLDI. 1994. *Injury, Collision, and Theft Losses by Make and Model.* Arlington, Va., Sept.

IIHS. 1994. Future of Crashworthiness Research Includes Frontal Offset Tests into a Deformable Barrier. *Status Report*, Vol. 29, No. 7, pp. 1–7.

IIHS. 1995a. Antilock Brakes Don't Reduce Crash Frequency or Cost, HLDI Reports. *Status Report*, Vol. 30, No. 2, Feb. 2, pp. 4–5.

IIHS. 1995b. European Union Moves Toward New Safety Standards with Dynamic Tests. *Status Report*, Vol. 30, No. 7, Aug. 12, p. 5.

IIHS. 1995c. IIHS Ranks Most Head Restraints "Poor" in Preventing Whiplash. *Highway and Vehicle Safety Report*, Vol. 22, No. 2, Oct. 2, pp. 5–6.

Kahane, C.J. 1982. *An Evaluation of Head Restraints, Federal Motor Vehicle Safety Standard 202.* DOT HS-806 108. NHTSA, U.S. Department of Transportation, Feb., 308 pp.

Kahane, C.J. 1994. *Correlation of NCAP Performance with Fatality Risk in Actual Head-On Collisions.* DOT-HS-808-061. National Highway Traffic Safety Administration, Jan., 164 pp.

Kahane, C.J., J.R. Hackney, and A.M Berkowitz. 1994. *Correlation of Vehicle Performance in the New Car Assessment Program with Fatality Risk in Actual Head-On Collisions.* Paper No. 94-S8-O-11. National Highway Traffic Safety Administration, 17 pp.

Lave, L.B. 1981. Conflicting Objectives in Regulating the Automobile. *Science*, Vol. 212, May 22, pp. 893–899.

Lund, A.K., and B. O'Neill. 1986. Perceived Risks and Driving Behavior. *Accident Analysis and Prevention*, Vol. 18, No. 5, pp. 367–370.

Machey, J.M., and C.L. Gauthier. 1984. Results, Analysis and Conclusions of NHTSA's 35 MPH Frontal Crash Test Repeatability Program. SAE Paper No. 840201. Society of Automotive Engineers, Warrendale, Pa., pp. 73–85.

Malliaris, A.C., and K.H. Digges. 1987. Crash Protection Offered by Safety Belts. *Proc., 11th International Conference on Safety Vehicles*, Washington, D.C.

McElhaney, J.H., and B.S. Myers. 1993. Biomechanical Aspects of Cervical Trauma. In *Accidental Injury: Biomechanics and Prevention* (A.M. Nahum and J.W. Melvin, eds.), Springer-Verlag, New York, pp. 311–361.

NHTSA. 1992. *Planning Document for Rollover Prevention and Injury Mitigation.* Docket 91-68. No. 1. Office of Vehicle Safety Standards, Sept., 13 pp.

NHTSA. 1993. *New Car Assessment Program.* Response to the NCAP FY 1992 Congressional Requirements. U.S. Department of Transportation, Dec., 125 pp.

NHTSA. 1994. *Traffic Safety Facts 1993.* DOT HS 808 169. U.S. Department of Transportation, Oct., 190 pp.

NHTSA. 1995. *The New Car Assessment Program.* Office of Market Incentives, U.S. Department of Transportation, 5 pp.

NRC. 1985. *Injury in America: A Continuing Public Health Problem.* National Academy Press, Washington, D.C., 164 pp.

Ollson, I., O. Bunketorp, G. Carlsson, C. Gustagfsson, I. Planath, H. Norin, and L. Yslander. 1990. An In-Depth Study of Neck Injuries in Rear End Collisions. *Proc., 1990 International IRCOBI Conference on the Biomechanics of Impacts,* Lyon, France, pp. 269–280.

O'Neill, B. 1995. *The Physics of Car Crashes and the Role of Vehicle Size and Weight in Occupant Protection.* Insurance Institute for Highway Safety, Arlington, Va., July, 14 pp.

Peltzman, S. 1975. The Effects of Automobile Safety Regulation. *Journal of Political Economy,* Vol. 83, Aug.–Dec., pp. 677–725.

Svenssan, M., P. Lōvsund, Y. Háland, and S. Larsson. 1993. Rear-End Collisions: A Study of the Influence of Backrest Properties on Head-Neck Motion Using a New Dummy Neck. Paper 93-343. Society of Automotive Engineers, Warrendale, Pa.

Syson, S.R. 1995. *Occupant to Roof Contact: Rollovers and Drop Tests. Advances in Occupant Protection Technologies for the Mid-Nineties.* SP1077. Society of Automotive Engineers, Warrendale, Pa., pp. 1–27.

TRB. 1988. *Special Report 218: Transportation in an Aging Society, Vol. 1.* National Research Council, Washington, D.C., 125 pp.

TRB. 1990. *Special Report 229: Safety Research for a Changing Highway Environment.* National Research Council, Washington, D.C., 166 pp.

Viano, D.C. 1987. Evaluation of the SID Dummy and TTI Injury Criterion for Side Impact Testing. No. 872208. *Proc., 31st Stapp Car Crash Conference,* Society of Automotive Engineers.

Viano, D.C., A. King, J.W. Melvin, and K. Weber. 1989. Injury Biomechanics Research: An Essential Element in the Prevention of Trauma. *Journal of Biomechanics,* Vol. 22, pp. 403–418.

Wilde, G.J.S. 1982. The Theory of Risk Homeostasis: Implications for Safety and Health. *Risk Analysis,* Vol. 2, No. 4, pp. 209–225.

Wolkomir, R. 1995. Sitting in Our Stead: Crash Dummies Take the Hard Knocks for All of Us. *Smithsonian,* Vol. 26, No. 4, July, pp. 30–41.

Yoganandan, N., F.A. Pintar, A. Sances, J.M. Reinhartz, and S.J. Larson. 1991. Strength and Kinematic Response of Dynamic Cervical Spine Injuries. *Spine,* Vol. 16, pp. 511–517.

# 3

## CURRENTLY AVAILABLE CONSUMER AUTOMOTIVE SAFETY INFORMATION

Considerable information about vehicle safety characteristics and features is available to consumers, but not always in a comparable or readily accessible form. An overview of the key sources of vehicle safety information and dissemination outlets through which information is currently made available to consumers is provided in this chapter. A critical assessment of the strengths and weaknesses of the information from the perspective of new car purchasers and a brief explanation of why there is limited market incentive to produce better data are given. Finally, improvements in both the substance and communication of vehicle safety information are suggested.

### SOURCES OF CONSUMER VEHICLE SAFETY INFORMATION

Consumers need comparative information on vehicle safety to help select a safer car. The following paragraphs highlight sources of comparative information in describing vehicle safety information currently provided by the government, nonprofit organizations, and the private sector (Table 3-1).

### Comparative Vehicle Safety Data

The New Car Assessment Program (NCAP) is the primary governmental consumer safety information program. Each year the National Highway Traffic Safety Administration (NHTSA) tests the frontal crash performance of a selected number of the most popular vehicles. Forty-one model year 1995 vehicles, representing passenger cars, pickup trucks, vans, and sport utility vehicles, were tested at three facilities (NHTSA 1995a, 1–2).[1]

TABLE 3-1    PRIMARY SOURCES OF COMPARATIVE
VEHICLE SAFETY INFORMATION

| INFORMATION SOURCE | TYPE OF INFORMATION | RATING CATEGORIES/ COMPARISONS |
|---|---|---|
| NHTSA | Frontal crash test (NCAP) results | Five stars/within vehicle class comparisons only |
| IIHS | Offset crash test results | Four rating categories/ within vehicle class comparisons only |
|  | Driver death rates | Indexed to average for all passenger vehicles/within and across vehicle class comparisons |
| HLDI | Injury, collision, and theft losses | Five rating categories indexed to average for all passenger vehicles/within and across vehicle class comparisons |
| CU | Braking and emergency handling tests (CU); frontal crash test results (NHTSA-NCAP); injury claim rates (HLDI) | Five rating categories/ within and across vehicle class comparisons except for crash test results |

Note: NHTSA = National Highway Traffic Safety Administration; NCAP = New Car Assessment Program; IIHS = Insurance Institute for Highway Safety; HLDI = Highway Loss Data Institute; CU = Consumers Union.

The first program of its kind to provide comparative information on vehicle crashworthiness, the NCAP was recently redesigned to provide more consumer-friendly information. Crash test results are now provided in a simplified star-rating system, which indicates worst (one star) to best (five stars) crash protection for vehicles in the same weight class (NHTSA 1995a, 1).

The Insurance Institute for Highway Safety (IIHS) published the results of offset frontal crash tests performed at its crash test facilities for the first time in 1995 (IIHS 1995a). The performance of each of 14 midsize, four-door cars for model year 1995 was compared and given an overall score on a four-point scale.[2] IIHS and the associated Highway Loss Data Institute (HLDI) also provide comparative data on the outcomes of vehicle crashes. IIHS compiles information on vehicle occupant fatalities by vehicle size and body style. Driver death rates for specific makes and models are compared with those of other vehicles in their class and with overall passenger vehicle driver death rates (IIHS 1995b).[3] HLDI compiles data on three insurance loss categories— injury, collision, and theft, standardized to reduce differences because of operator age and deductible amount (HLDI 1995).[4] The results are rated according to five categories and grouped by vehicle size and body style. In 1995 NHTSA required dealers to provide prospective buyers with HLDI-generated comparative information on collision losses by vehicle make and model.[5] The comparative data provided by IIHS and HLDI provide consumers with useful information about real-world crash experience. However, when new model designs are introduced, they do not provide new car buyers with prospective information. Nor do they isolate the vehicle-related characteristics contributing to crash likelihood and crash outcomes from the driver and environmental characteristics.

Perhaps the best-known source of new car information is *Consumer Reports*. Consumers Union (CU) runs its own tests of such vehicle safety characteristics as emergency handling and braking performance. Other comparative safety information is drawn from several external sources, including manufacturer-provided data on vehicle safety features and equipment, NHTSA-provided NCAP ratings, and insurance industry-provided data on injury claim rates and insurance costs. These safety data have been modified to fit within *Consumer Reports'* typical five rating categories.

The automobile manufacturers provide a wide range of consumer-oriented safety information, including details on new car labels about specific vehicle safety features such as air bags and antilock brakes, safety information in owner's manuals, and videos and cassettes showing vehicle handling and performance characteristics and the operation of specific safety features. The information is useful for owners of new vehicles but provides little in the way of comparative data to assist consumers in making purchase decisions.

Safety advocacy groups also provide consumer information. For example, the American Coalition for Traffic Safety, Inc., has developed several brochures providing consumers with information on such vehicle safety features as air bags and antilock brakes and on ways to prevent such crash types as rollovers. None of these publications, however, provide comparative vehicle safety information.

## Summary Compilations of Vehicle Safety Information

Several publications are available in which an attempt is made to compile comparative vehicle safety information in one place for distribution to consumers. CU publishes passenger car and light truck vehicle evaluations in the issues of its monthly magazine, *Consumer Reports*, which include a summary of safety information for each vehicle. Its April issue is devoted entirely to cars and light truck vehicles and provides detailed comparisons of hundreds of new and used vehicles, including all available safety information. In addition, CU publishes an annual *New Car Yearbook* and *New Car Buying Guide*. *The New Car Yearbook*, as an example, provides summary automotive safety information and evaluations of performance, cost, and features in single-page vehicle profiles (Figure 3-1).

*The Car Book* by Jack Gillis is another comprehensive source of information, including safety information, about new cars.[6] A separate chapter on safety includes information on safety features and vehicle crashworthiness. NCAP crash test results, which are organized by vehicle class, are presented in several different ways—a numerical injury index, a five-category rating, and a probability-of-injury outcome rating. Other publications, including the American Automobile Association's (AAA's) *Auto Test*, Consumer Guide's automobile ratings, and automobile magazines such as *Car and Driver*, also provide comprehensive new car information, but with much less emphasis on safety.[7]

NHTSA and IIHS have produced small brochures that provide comparative information focused primarily on vehicle safety. NHTSA's recently developed consumer guide, *Buying a Safer Car*, was cosponsored by AAA and the Federal Trade Commission. The guide provides several safety buying tips. Vehicle-specific information follows on such topics as availability of safety features (i.e., driver and passenger air bags, antilock brakes, adjustable seat belt anchors, and 1997 side-impact protection), crash test results, and theft ratings, organized by vehicle class.

IIHS has developed a booklet entitled *Shopping for a Safer Car* that introduces the consumer to such basic safety concepts as vehicle size

Medium car

# Buick Century

This dated design is seriously outclassed by the competition. Its one notable virtue is a better-than-average reliability record. Every little twist in the road makes the car lean heavily and squeal its tires. The ride feels spongy, with hopping, wallowing, and bouncing on bumpy roads. The current Century is big on the outside but cramped inside. Even some small sedans such as the Mazda Protegé and Chrysler's Dodge/Plymouth Neon have more room in the rear seat. The controls are overstyled and inconveniently placed. The optional 3.1-liter V6 and four-speed automatic make a much better choice than the standard 2.2-liter Four and three-speed automatic, but you're even better off choosing a different model. Our comments on the sedan apply to the station wagon as well.

| Body styles and prices | | |
|---|---|---|
| | **Price range** | **Trim lines** |
| 4-door | $16,720-$19,406 | Special, Custom, Limited |
| 4-door wagon | $18,135 | Special |

### KEY FOR CRASH-PROTECTION JUDGMENTS

- ● Probably no injury or a minor injury
- ◑ Moderate injury likely
- ○ Certain injury, possibly severe
- ◔ Severe or fatal injury highly likely
- ● Severe or fatal injury virtually certain

### KEY FOR INJURY CLAIM RATES

●   ◑   ○   ◔   ●

Much better  ←——————→  Much worse
than average       than average

| Safety information | |
|---|---|
| Driver air bag | Standard |
| Passenger air bag | Not offered |
| Antilock brakes | Standard |
| Traction control | Not offered |
| Side-impact protection claimed | No |
| Driver crash protection | ● |
| Passenger crash protection | ○ |
| Injury claim rate compared with all cars | ◔ |
| Injury claim rate compared with medium cars | ● |

| Reliability history | | | | | | | | |
|---|---|---|---|---|---|---|---|---|
| **TROUBLE SPOTS** | **Buick Century** | | | | | | | |
| | 87 | 88 | 89 | 90 | 91 | 92 | 93 | 94 |
| Engine | ◑ | ● | ◑ | ◑ | ● | ● | ● | ● |
| Cooling | ◑ | ● | ○ | ○ | ◑ | ● | ◑ | ◑ |
| Fuel | ◑ | ● | ○ | ◑ | ● | ◑ | ● | ● |
| Ignition | ○ | ○ | ○ | ● | ● | ● | ● | ● |
| Auto. transmission | ○ | ● | ◑ | ◑ | ◑ | ● | ● | ◑ |
| Man. transmission | | | | | | | | |
| Clutch | | | | | | | | |
| Electrical | ● | ● | ◑ | ○ | ○ | ◑ | ○ | ◑ |
| Air-conditioning | ○ | ○ | ◑ | ● | ◑ | ● | ● | ◑ |
| Suspension | ◑ | ○ | ◑ | ● | ◑ | ● | ● | ● |
| Brakes | ● | ● | ● | ● | ◑ | ○ | ○ | ● |
| Exhaust | ◑ | ● | ◑ | ◑ | ● | ◑ | ● | ● |
| Body rust | ◑ | ○ | ◑ | ● | ● | ● | ◑ | ● |
| Paint/trim | ● | ● | ◑ | ◑ | ◑ | ● | ◑ | ● |
| Body integrity | ○ | ○ | ○ | ○ | ● | ◑ | ○ | ◑ |
| Body hardware | ● | ◑ | ○ | ○ | ○ | ◑ | ◑ | ◑ |

| Test judgments | |
|---|---|
| **Performance** | |
| Acceleration | ○ |
| Transmission | ◔ |
| Routine handling | ◑ |
| Emergency handling | ◑ |
| Braking | ○ |
| **Comfort** | |
| Ride, normal load | ○ |
| Ride, full load | ○ |
| Noise | ◑ |
| Driving position | ◑ |
| Front-seat comfort | ◑ |
| Rear-seat comfort | ◑ |
| Climate-control system | ◔ |
| **Convenience** | |
| Access | ○ |
| Controls and displays | ● |
| Trunk | ◔ |
| **Other** | |
| Fuel economy | ○ |
| Predicted reliability | ◑ |
| Predicted depreciation | ◔ |

## Test data

| Acceleration | | Fuel economy | | Braking from 60 mph | |
|---|---|---|---|---|---|
| 0-30 mph, sec. | 3.6 | Type of fuel | Regular | Dry pavement, ft. | 144 |
| 0-60 mph, sec. | 10.1 | EPA city/highway, mpg | 19/29 | Wet pavement, ft. | 155 |
| Quarter mile, sec. | 17.6 | CU's city/highway, mpg | 14/36 | Pedal effort, 1st stop, lb. | 20 |
| Quarter mile, mph | 81 | CU's overall mileage, mpg | 22 | Pedal effort, 10th stop, lb. | 30 |
| 45-65 mph, sec. | 6.7 | CU's 150-mile trip, mpg | 28 | | |
| | | Fuel refill capacity, gal. | 16.5 | | |
| | | Cruising range, mi. | 425 | | |
| | | Annual fuel: gal./cost | 690/$825 | | |

## Specifications

| Drive wheels | | Interior room | | Engines available | |
|---|---|---|---|---|---|
| Front | | Front shoulder room, in. | 56.5 | 2.2-liter 4 (120 hp) | |
| **Seating** | | Front leg room, in. | 41.0 | 3.1-liter V6 (160 hp) | |
| Max. passengers | 3/3 | Front head room, in. | 4.0 | | |
| **Dimensions and weight** | | Rear shoulder room, in. | 56.0 | **Transmissions available** | |
| Length, in. | 189 | Rear fore-aft room, in. | 25.5 | 3- or 4-speed automatic | |
| Width, in. | 69 | Rear head room, in. | 2.5 | **Tested model** | |
| Wheelbase, in. | 105 | Door top to ground, in. | 50.5 | Special, 3.1-liter V6, 4-speed automatic | |
| Turning circle, ft. | 43 | Luggage capacity | 5+2 | | |
| Curb weight, lb. | 3100 | | | | |
| Percent weight, front/rear | 66/34 | | | | |
| Max. load, lb. | 1063 | | | | |

**KEY: SAFETY INFORMATION**
Safety equipment includes **air bags, antilock brakes,** and **traction control,** as specified by manufacturers. Some automakers now state that their cars meet a new safety standard for improved side-impact protection. All passenger cars will have to comply with that standard by 1997.
    **Crash-protection scores** come from our analysis of Government 35-mph barrier crash tests, which simulate a head-on crash with a similar vehicle approaching at the same speed. Instrumented and safety-belted "driver" and "passenger" dummies record the crash forces.
    **Injury claim rates** are based on frequency of insurance claims, as reported by the Highway Loss Data Institute, an independent group supported by the insurance industry. Only cars whose design and safety restraints are like those of the 1996 models are included. Rates are shown compared with the average of all vehicles in the database and with the average for similar vehicles. The latter comparison is more likely to focus on the car rather than the driver.

**FIGURE 3-1   Example of comparative vehicle safety information provided by Consumers Union (*1996 New Car Yearbook*). Note: edited for illustrative purposes.**

and structure. Various safety features are highlighted (dual air bags, side-impact protection, head and child restraints), and cars that have well-designed features are identified. The brochure directs consumers to other safety information sources, such as crash test results.

Individual insurance companies also provide summary vehicle safety information to their policyholders. For example, the United Services Automotive Association (USAA), the nations' sixth-largest insurer of motor vehicles, publishes a booklet entitled *The Car Guide*. The guide provides a vehicle safety and insurance "report card" on specific vehicles organized by manufacturer. Performance ratings are given for crash test results, fatality rates, injury frequency and collision loss, theft loss, and claims experience.

This brief overview indicates that some comparative vehicle safety information is available to consumers. As discussed in the following section, however, consumers must be knowledgeable and diligent to access the information and give it proper consideration.

## DISSEMINATION OUTLETS

Little comparative vehicle safety information is available at the dealership (Table 3-2). Safety features, such as antilock brakes and air bags, are mentioned on new car vehicle labels along with many other features. More detailed information about the operation of safety features is contained in owner's manuals. The only comparative safety information is the booklet on differences in collision losses that NHTSA now requires all dealers to make available to prospective new car purchasers.

More information is available to consumers before they go to the showroom (Table 3-2), but obtaining comparable safety data on a wide range of vehicles is difficult. *Consumer Reports* has a wide circulation. Nearly 5 million subscribers receive this publication, including libraries, and nonsubscription sales are large.[8] The *New Car Yearbook* is for sale on the newsstands in the fall, and *New Car Buying Guide* is sold by mail, in bookstores, and on newsstands. The same data are provided to consumers by the major commercial on-line services—America On Line, CompuServe, and Prodigy. Finally, CU recently published a CD-ROM entitled *Consumer Reports Cars: The Essential Guide*. With average sales of about 75,000 per year, Jack Gillis's *The Car Book* reaches a smaller but still significant audience.

NHTSA has recently increased the visibility of its NCAP crash test results in response to a congressional request to revamp the communi-

**TABLE 3-2   PRIMARY DISSEMINATION OUTLETS FOR CONSUMER VEHICLE SAFETY INFORMATION**

| DISSEMINATOR | TYPE OF COMMUNICATION | MODE | FREQUENCY |
|---|---|---|---|
| **Point-of-Sale Information** | | | |
| Automobile manufacturers | New car label[a] (list of safety features) | Print | N.A. |
| | Owner's manual[a] | Print | N.A. |
| NHTSA | Collision loss booklet | Print | Annual |
| **Presale Information** | | | |
| CU | Magazine: *Consumer Reports* | Print and on-line | Monthly |
| | Magazine: *New Car Yearbook* | Print | Annual |
| | Book: *New Car Buying Guide* | Print | Annual |
| | CD-ROM: *Consumer Reports Cars: The Essential Guide* | Electronic | Periodic |
| AAA/NHTSA | Brochure: *Buying a Safer Car* | Print | Periodic |

| | | | |
|---|---|---|---|
| NHTSA | Pamphlet: NCAP test results | Print and electronic (through NHTSA hotline) | Periodic releases throughout the year |
| IIHS | Booklet: Offset frontal crash test results | Print (publicized through *NBC Dateline*) | Periodic |
| | Pamphlet: *Shopping for a Safer Car* | Print | Annual |
| | Special Issue: *Death Rates by Vehicle Make, Series* | Print | Annual |
| HLDI | Pamphlet: *Injury, Collision, and Theft Losses* | Print | Annual |

Note: N.A. = not appropriate; NHTSA = National Highway Traffic Safety Administration; CU = Consumers Union; AAA = American Automobile Association; NCAP = New Car Assessment Program; IIHS = Insurance Institute for Highway Safety; HLDI = Highway Loss Data Institute.

[a]No comparative information.

cations aspect of the program. In addition to regular press releases, the agency inaugurated a hotline in 1994 through which electronic or printed versions of the crash test results are made available. Approximately 35,000 requests for NCAP data were received through the hotline in 1994 (NHTSA 1995a, 3). NHTSA may achieve wider circulation of NCAP test results from its new consumer guide, *Buying a Safer Car*, which incorporates the NCAP test results and is available through AAA as well as the NHTSA hotline.[9] Finally, NCAP test scores are picked up in both *The New Car Yearbook* and *The Car Book*.

Consumer-oriented comparative vehicle safety information is also available in the summary brochures and special reports from IIHS and HLDI described earlier.[10] Consumers, however, must know where to call to receive these publications. A few individual insurers like USAA send out comparative vehicle safety information with their premium notices. IIHS itself recently launched its offset frontal crash testing program with a highly visible NBC *Dateline* presentation, which resulted in numerous requests for its consumer-oriented booklet summarizing the test results.[11]

This brief overview of communication modes and dissemination outlets for consumer vehicle safety information suggests that the information is scattered among several providers. Little comparative information is available at the dealership. More presale information is available, much of it in print form—special magazine issues, brochures, and pamphlets. With the exception of *Consumer Reports* and perhaps *The Car Book*, however, which are widely known, consumers may not be aware of the publications or where to obtain the information.

## DEVELOPMENT OF THE NCAP STAR-RATING SYSTEM: A CASE STUDY

Recent efforts to develop a more consumer-oriented presentation and communication of NCAP test results provide a good illustration of the difficulties involved in the development of meaningful consumer automotive safety information.

In fiscal year 1992 the Senate and Conference Appropriations Reports requested that NHTSA implement improved methods to inform consumers of the comparative crashworthiness of passenger vehicles as measured by NCAP crash test results.[12] Up to that time, NHTSA had simply published numerical injury scores indicating the likelihood of head, chest, and upper leg injuries. Responding to focus groups calling for presentation of the crash test information "in a form that is non-technical and as short and simple as possible," NHTSA developed a new star-rating format and inaugurated a hotline through which consumers could request the information (NHTSA 1993, 43, 58).

Beginning with model year 1994 vehicles, the new rating system combines the head and chest injury crash test scores into a single rating of one to five stars, one star indicating the least crash protection for drivers and front seat passengers and five the most.[13] The number of stars relates to the probability of serious injury. One star is equivalent to a 45 percent or greater chance of sustaining a serious injury in a frontal crash, and five stars is equivalent to a 10 percent chance of sustaining a serious injury. This information on injury likelihood, however, is not given to the consumer. A brief cover sheet provides basic information about the crash test and reiterates that the results should be used only to compare vehicles in the same weight class. Specific vehicles are then grouped by weight and rated accordingly.

The new rating system provides consumers with a more readily understandable summary measure of vehicle occupant protection in frontal crashes than the old numerical scoring system.[14] At the same time it has raised several concerns, many from the safety community. The first set of concerns relates to the presentation of the information. Some critics maintain that the use of stars as rating symbols is inappropriate. The public generally associates stars with good performance. Yet a one-star NCAP rating means a 45 percent or greater probability of sustaining a serious injury. In the critics' view, vehicles that receive this rating should not receive a star or should have a negative rating (IIHS 1995c, 3).

A related concern is the technical basis for selecting five rating categories. Critics maintain that the star system translates relatively small differences in injury criteria into what can be perceived as more major differences—for example, three stars versus four. There appears to be no statistical evidence that the differences in the ratings are systematically related to differences in crashworthiness (IIHS 1995c, 3).[15] In fact, an analysis of model year 1995 ratings suggests that most cars fall within a narrower rating band of three to five stars, although light trucks, vans, and sport utility vehicles exhibit a more even distribution among the five categories (Figure 3-2).[16] Furthermore, no estimate is provided of the variance within each rating category, a nontrivial issue.

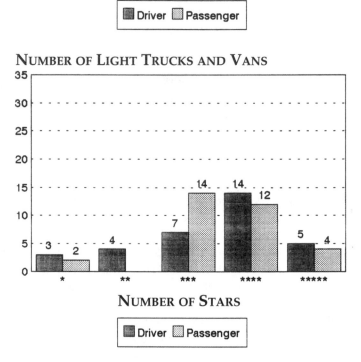

**NUMBER OF CARS**

**NUMBER OF STARS**

Driver Passenger

**NUMBER OF LIGHT TRUCKS AND VANS**

**NUMBER OF STARS**

Driver Passenger

FIGURE 3-2   NCAP star ratings of the frontal crashworthiness of passenger cars (above) and light trucks, sport utility vehicles, and vans (below), model year 1995 (NHTSA 1995c).

Large variances in individual test scores that underlie the ratings because of vehicle or test differences could render distinctions among the rating categories meaningless.

A final set of concerns relates to the potential for the star ratings to mislead. For example, consumers may compare ratings for vehicles in different weight classes, which is not valid. For example, they may conclude erroneously that a small compact with a five-star rating is as generally crashworthy as a large sedan with a similar rating. NHTSA warns the consumer against making such comparisons in its literature and groups vehicle ratings by vehicle weight class. This caveat can easily be overlooked, however, when vehicles and related rating information are listed alphabetically or by manufacturer, as they are in several consumer guides. Consumers may make the same mistake if numerical scores are provided, but the simplified star-rating scheme makes it even easier to mistakenly compare scores across car classes (IIHS 1994, 4).

## STRENGTHS AND WEAKNESSES OF CURRENT INFORMATION

As the NCAP star-rating system illustrates, providing consumers with meaningful, yet not misleading, comparative information is a challenge.

The available information, although limited, gives consumers some basis on which to compare vehicle safety. Most of the literature identifies passenger vehicles that have desirable safety features. Of course, once the vehicle is purchased, much information is available from owner's manuals and safety advocacy groups about how to use these safety features.

Consumers can also use NCAP ratings to compare the frontal crashworthiness of vehicles within the same weight class. As indicated in the preceding chapter, there is evidence that the underlying test scores have some correlation with differences in real-world crash performance, at least for vehicles that rank at the top or the bottom of the rating scale.[17]

Finally, consumers can use IIHS and HLDI data to examine real-world outcomes, such as driver and occupant fatalities, by vehicle make and model. Death rates, however, are influenced by driver characteristics and driving conditions as well as vehicle design.

Another frequently overlooked benefit of consumer information is the incentive provided to manufacturers to improve the safety design of vehicles. The NCAP is a case in point. NCAP scores have improved steadily since the inception of the program, with the largest improvement in the early years. Most passenger cars now meet the lower [48-km/hr (30-mph)] regulatory standard at the higher [56-km/hr (35-mph)] NCAP test speed. The results are not as good for light trucks, vans, and sport utility vehicles, because crashworthiness standards were phased in later for light truck vehicles than for cars (Kahane et al. 1994, 13). Improvements in test performance have been matched by real-world reductions in fatality likelihood for drivers in head-on crashes similar to those simulated by the NCAP test.[18] The NCAP is not the sole stimulus for this improvement in safety; the 1984 regulations leading to automatic passenger restraint systems and air bags were another important factor. But the program can claim part of the credit.

Given all the data listed earlier, why do consumers not have adequate information on which to compare and make choices about vehicle safety? Several reasons are apparent. First, there are critical gaps in current information. Most significant, the important role of vehicle weight and size in crash outcomes is not emphasized in consumer safety literature, with the exception of the IIHS brochure *Shopping for a Safer Car*.

Comparative safety information is also limited for vehicles within the same size and weight class. For example, NCAP crash protection ratings reflect vehicle crashworthiness for only one very limited crash type—head-on collisions. No comparative information is available about how vehicles perform in side-impact crashes and rollovers, two crash types resulting in significant numbers of fatalities. IIHS has begun to rate vehicle crashworthiness in offset crash tests, representing a more common type of frontal crash. The rating categories are different from the NCAP system. Moreover, the probability of head and chest injury measured by the two tests may differ. This result is not surprising because the tests measure different aspects of vehicle crashworthiness.[19] In fact, one could argue that testing more crash types is beneficial because it encourages manufacturers to optimize safety design for more crash types. However, explaining these differences in any detail, or simply presenting the results without explanation, is likely to confuse the consumer.

The results of comparing information from crash tests with real-world crash data for the same vehicle are frequently, but not always, consistent. For example, a comparison of the NCAP crash test ratings with actual fatality rates for the four-door Ford Escort, a popular car in the small car category, provides conflicting information. The 1995 model year Ford Escort receives a four-star NCAP rating for both driver and front seat passenger, only one star below the highest rating. Yet real-world crash data indicate a driver death rate about 50 percent higher than for other vehicles in its class. Similar results can be shown for Chevrolet's 1995 model year Geo Metro four-door sedan (NHTSA 1995c; IIHS 1995b). Part of the difference may be attributed to the use of dual air bag-equipped cars for model year 1995 NCAP tests. Crash test results for 1990–1993 were based on belt-equipped vehicles. Part of the difference may reflect the influence of driver and vehicle use characteristics in the crash data. These distinctions serve to highlight the difficulties that consumers may find in attempting to reconcile such information.

Where an attempt is made to bring safety data together in one place (e.g., CU's *New Car Yearbook, New Car Buying Guide,* and CD-ROM *Consumer Reports Cars: The Essential Guide;* NHTSA's *Buying a Safer Car;* IIHS's *Shopping for a Safer Car;* USAA's *Car Guide*), the information available to the public is often incomplete. Missing NCAP ratings are most noticeable, reflecting the relatively small number of vehicles tested and the timing of the release of test results, which is not necessarily coordinated with consumer or insurance industry publication deadlines. (Test dates can also vary widely, particularly for test results from prior years for models that have not changed substantially.) It is clear that the public would benefit from an increased number of models evaluated in the NCAP. *Consumer Reports* also does not rate every automobile yearly. Finally, even when the information is available, consumers are not always provided an explanation of the limited predictive power of the crash tests generally, the certainty of the ratings themselves, or how to combine the information.

In summary, information is available that enables consumers to compare the safety performance of different vehicles, but much more could be done to make the information more comprehensive and easier for consumers to interpret and use.

## WHY BETTER INFORMATION IS NOT PROVIDED

When considering the need for improvements in information about vehicle safety, one could ask why such information is not being provided by the market, particularly if consumer interest in automotive safety information is growing. The answer lies in part in the nature of the information. Product safety information is a typical example of what economists call a "public good." The defining property of a public good is that, once the good is provided, the consumption of that good by one individual does not diminish its availability for consumption by others (Rosen 1995, 61). A related characteristic is the difficulty of excluding those who are not willing to pay for consuming the good (Rosen 1995, 62). Thus, a consumer does not have an incentive to pay the full cost of obtaining the information and can become a "free rider."[20] As a result, firms providing information are unable to capture through their pricing the full value of their informational product to consumers. Thus they will provide less information than what consumers in the aggregate would be willing to pay for—an amount that an efficient market would supply.

The insurance industry (through IIHS and HLDI) and CU provide comparative vehicle safety information for which consumers are willing to pay—directly in the case of CU and indirectly through insurance premiums in the case of the insurance industry. However, the large expense of crash testing—the capital expense of establishing a test facility and operating costs of approximately $15,000 per test plus the cost of the vehicle—is a barrier to any one organization conducting multiple tests per vehicle on the full range of vehicles available each year necessary to develop comprehensive comparative summary data. For example, CU regularly conducts tests on a wide range of products, but, as a nonprofit consumer organization, it could not absorb or recover the added costs of a complete crash testing program for passenger cars and light truck vehicles. In accord with its mission, CU publications are widely available to the public in libraries and through the media, which publicize CU's information, thus exacerbating the free rider problem.

The insurance industry has funded a state-of-the-art crash test facility and begun an offset crash testing program, now being expanded. Here, too, the industry on its own, even through a pooled effort, cannot hope to recoup the cost of a major expansion of its crash testing program, in part because of the free rider problem and in part because of the structure of regulated rates, which are not closely linked with the crash performance or safety records of insured vehicles. Moreover, the direct benefits to automobile insurers from safer vehicles are affected by the tort liability system in effect in most states. Payments for injuries to "third parties" (occupants of other vehicles, pedestrians, bicyclists), not to the occupants of the vehicles they insure, are the largest injury-related claims costs for insurers.

Finally, the automobile manufacturers conduct crash tests to meet regulatory standards, but test results are proprietary. The manufacturers also face significant barriers to providing accurate comprehensive comparative safety data to consumers. The cost of testing would be high relative to the benefits that any one company would receive and consumers might perceive the test results to be biased toward the cars sold by that company. To date, NHTSA has paid for the major crash test program, NCAP, that provides consumers with crash test data.

It is probably for these reasons that the market has failed to provide more comprehensive comparative safety information and that public funds have supported the NCAP. A cost-sharing approach involving the insurance and automobile industries and NHTSA could help provide the incentives and the resources to conduct the necessary crash tests and produce the comparative information.

## MAKING BETTER USE OF EXISTING INFORMATION

The presentation and communication of existing consumer vehicle safety information could be improved in a number of ways. First, critical factors that affect vehicle safety should be highlighted in consumer safety publications. For example, the important relationship between vehicle size and weight and occupant protection is well understood but needs to be more prominently featured in consumer-oriented safety publications. Second, common misconceptions about use of vehicle safety features should be addressed. For example, it should be made clear that antilock brakes should not be pumped and that air bags do not replace seat belts.

Third, further improvements could be made in the government's primary consumer safety information program, NCAP. Much time and effort have gone into reviews of the program, particularly the new star-rating system, but many issues remain unresolved. Several organizations have questioned the use of the star symbol and the basis for the selection of rating categories (NHTSA 1995d; IIHS 1995c). If the star symbol is retained, consumers should at least be provided information about the outcomes (i.e., likelihood of injury) associated with each rating category. They should also be given information on the frequency of the frontal crashes that the crash tests represent.

Fourth, questions about the reliability of the underlying test data persist. These concerns may best be met by a new study, which would attempt to document the variance from test to test and the sources of that variance. Such a study was recommended by the General Accounting Office in its recent report (GAO 1995, 9).[21]

Fifth, conducting crash tests at different speeds and for other than frontal crashes could provide consumers with more comprehensive crashworthiness data than are currently available, but expansion of crash testing is highly controversial. The manufacturers oppose any expansion of crash testing until the reliability of the new test modes and correlation with real-world crashes are better understood (NHTSA 1995d, 18–20). Safety groups, in contrast, believe that NCAP should continue to be a cutting-edge program. Thus, new crash tests should be considered to provide incentives for industry to improve vehicle performance in other than full-frontal crash types (NHTSA 1995d, 20–21). Offset crash tests are the most likely candidate in the near term. IIHS is gaining experience from its offset crash testing program, the Australians are conducting both full-frontal and offset crash tests for consumer information, and the European Union will soon introduce offset crash testing (NHTSA 1995d, 26; IIHS 1995d, 5). If information is shared, the results of these efforts could be sufficient to support an expanded offset crash testing program in the United States. As discussed in Chapter 2, introduction of consumer information programs on vehicle crashworthiness in side-impact and rollover crashes is probably premature. In the long run, entirely different types of crash tests may be developed using advanced computer techniques.

Finally, providers of vehicle safety information could improve the presentation and dissemination of information to the extent funding permits. Current efforts to compile summary information in one place, such as CU's *New Car Yearbook*, *New Car Buying Guide*, and CD-ROM *Consumer Reports Cars: The Essential Guide*; Jack Gillis's *The Car Book*; and the NHTSA and IIHS brochures, should be continued. Improvements in the structure and format of brochures and print documents currently published could be made, with empirical evaluation and systematic application of principles from research on text comprehension (Kintsch 1986; Ericsson 1988; Schriver 1989; Atman et al. 1994). These publications could also be made more accessible and available to consumers. More information could be made available electronically. More general access to the media can be accomplished by staging newsworthy events (Maibach and Holtgrave 1995, 227), such as IIHS's offset crash tests, which were broadcast on NBC's *Dateline*. Of course, advertising the availability of vehicle safety information (e.g., through public service announcements and consumer magazine inserts) should increase consumer awareness of the information's existence and of where and how it can be obtained.

Even with all these improvements, consumers are still likely to have difficulty integrating available information into a summary assessment of the relative safety of various vehicles in a form that serves their needs. Much more could be done to provide consumers with summary measures of overall vehicle safety that are easier to interpret and use in making purchase decisions. Development of more comprehensive information requires a better understanding of what consumers believe about safety and how they consider safety in the process of choosing a new vehicle, the subject of the following chapter.

## NOTES

1. Published information also includes ratings from prior years for models that were not substantially changed.
2. Using the same four-point scale, the cars were also rated on their structural performance; effectiveness of the occupant restraint systems; injury likelihood, including measures of head, neck, chest, and leg injury; head restraint design; and bumper performance (IIHS 1995a).
3. Fatality rates are drawn from NHTSA's Fatal Accident Reporting System, and vehicle registration counts come from R.L. Polk.
4. Operator age is based on the age of the "rated driver." The rated driver and the actual driver involved in a claim are not always the same.
5. The information reflects the average collision loss payment per insured vehicle year, which is presented as an index with 100 representing the average for all passenger vehicles (NHTSA 1995b, 1). The rating provides a measure of a vehicle's damage susceptibility, which only indirectly relates to its safety performance.
6. Separate books are available for passenger cars and for trucks, vans, and sport utility vehicles.
7. *Auto Test*, for example, does not include NCAP crash test results, although these may be found in the brochure AAA cosponsors with NHTSA entitled *Buying a Safer Car*.
8. CU estimates that the *New Car Yearbook* reaches about 14 million individuals if nonsubscription sales and indirect dissemination channels (e.g., libraries) are taken into account (personal communication, David Pittle, Consumers Union, Oct. 23, 1995).
9. For each brochure it disseminates, NHTSA must pay 50 cents. The copies are distributed from the National Consumer Information Center in Pueblo, Colorado, a repository of consumer information from all federal agencies.
10. For example, in 1995 there were requests for about 140,000 copies of IIHS's *Shopping for a Safer Car* and about the same number for HLDI's *Injury, Collision, and Theft Losses*. Copies of both of these publications were also distributed by sponsoring insurance companies, either under the name of the company or that of IIHS or HLDI.
11. IIHS's publications office estimated that it received 18,000 to 20,000 requests for the publication summarizing offset test results. Most requests followed the NBC *Dateline* presentation.

12. The reports also requested a study of the validity of the test data and the efficacy of allowing manufacturers to choose between "high-tech" and "low-tech" dummies for the purposes of NCAP testing (NHTSA 1993).

13. The star system relates head and chest injury test scores to injury probabilities using injury risk functions developed by biomechanical experts from the Ford Motor Company and General Motors Corporation. The risk functions relate the dummy measurements to injury probabilities (Hackney and Kahane 1995, 1). To calculate the injury probability rating, the head and chest scores are combined (although each is treated as an independent event), because an individual who suffers multiple injuries is likely to have a higher risk of permanent disability or death (Hackney and Kahane 1995, 2). Upper leg loads were not included because femur injury is seldom life threatening (Hackney and Kahane 1995, 2).

14. The numerical scores are published and made available to consumers on request.

15. In the judgment of agency staff, five rating categories were needed. Three did not provide enough variation, and four did not give a midpoint (personal communication, James Hackney, NHTSA, Aug. 10, 1995).

16. The analysis includes the 41 tested model year 1995 vehicles plus results from previous years for tested vehicle types that have not changed.

17. The researchers cautioned that the findings apply on the average. There is no guarantee that every specific make-model with a very poor NCAP score or, alternatively, an excellent score has a higher- or lower-than-average fatality risk, respectively, in head-on collisions (Kahane et al. 1994, 13).

18. The researchers found a 20 to 25 percent reduction in fatality risk for belted drivers in actual head-on collisions in model years 1979 through 1991, with the largest decreases during the early 1980s (Kahane et al. 1994, 13).

19. Full-frontal tests are more demanding of occupant restraint systems, whereas offset crash tests are more demanding of the structural integrity of the occupant compartment. For a more detailed explanation, see Chapter 2.

20. The importance of the free rider problem is an empirical question. For example, consumers purchase *Consumer Reports*, and their insurance companies, acting as their agents, pay for product safety information. The contributions of the insurance companies to IIHS and HLDI are examples of how a public good can be paid for in a market economy.

21. GAO recommended an update of the NCAP test variability study that NHTSA conducted in 1982 (see Chapter 2 for more details about that study).

## REFERENCES

### Abbreviations

| | |
|---|---|
| IIHS | Insurance Institute for Highway Safety |
| GAO | General Accounting Office |
| HLDI | Highway Loss Data Institute |
| NHTSA | National Highway Traffic Safety Administration |

Atman, C.J., A. Bostrom, B. Fischhoff, and M.G. Morgan. 1994. Designing Risk Communications: Completing and Correcting Mental Models of Hazardous Processes, Part I. *Risk Analysis*, Vol. 14, No. 5, pp. 779–788.

Ericsson, K.A. 1988. Concurrent Verbal Reports on Text Comprehension. *Text*, Vol. 8, No. 4, pp. 295–325.

GAO. 1995. *Highway Safety: Reliability and Validity of DOT Crash Tests.* GAO/ PEMD-95-5. May, 76 pp.

Hackney, J.R., and C.J. Kahane. 1995. The New Car Assessment Program: Five Star Rating System and Vehicle Safety Performance Characteristics. No. 950888. Presented at Society of Automotive Engineers International Congress and Exposition, Detroit, Mich., 16 pp.

HLDI. 1995. *Injury, Collision, and Theft Losses by Make and Model.* Arlington, Va., Sept.

IIHS. 1994. Future of NCAP: NHTSA Mulls Options To Expand Crash Test Program. *Status Report*, Vol. 29, No. 7, June 25, pp. 4–5.

IIHS. 1995a. *Crashworthiness Evaluations.* Arlington, Va.

IIHS. 1995b. Special Issue: Driver Death Rates by Vehicle Make, Series. *Status Report*, Vol. 30, No. 9, Oct. 14.

IIHS. 1995c. NCAP's Star Ratings Simply Don't Work, Safety and Consumer Groups Advise NHTSA. *Status Report*, Vol. 30, No. 1, Jan. 14, p. 3.

IIHS. 1995d. European Union Moves Toward New Safety Standards with Dynamic Tests. *Status Report*, Vol. 30, No. 7, Aug. 12.

Kahane, C.J., J.R. Hackney, and A.M. Berkowitz. 1994. *Correlation of Vehicle Performance in the New Car Assessment Program with Fatality Risk in Actual Head-On Collisions.* Paper No. 94-S8-O-11. National Highway Traffic Safety Administration, 17 pp.

Kintsch, W. 1986. Learning from Text. *Cognition and Instruction*, Vol. 3, pp. 87–108.

Maibach, E., and D.R. Holtgrave.1995. Advances in Public Health Communication. *Annual Review of Public Health*, Vol. 16, pp. 219–238.

NHTSA. 1993. *New Car Assessment Program.* Response to the NCAP FY 1992 Congressional Requirements. U.S. Department of Transportation, Dec., 125 pp.

NHTSA. 1995a. *The New Car Assessment Program.* Office of Market Incentives, U.S. Department of Transportation, 5 pp.

NHTSA. 1995b. *Comparison of Differences in Insurance Costs for Passenger Motor Vehicles on the Basis of Damage Susceptibility.* U.S. Department of Transportation, Feb., 10 pp.

NHTSA. 1995c. *New Car Assessment Program, Test Results, Model Year 1995.* U.S. Department of Transportation, May, 10 pp.

NHTSA. 1995d. *New Car Assessment Program Public Meeting.* U.S. Department of Transportation, Feb., 28 pp.

Rosen, H.S. 1995. *Public Finance* (4th ed.). Richard D. Irwin, Inc.

Schriver, K. 1989. Evaluating Text Quality: The Continuum from Text-Focused to Reader-Focused Methods. *IEEE Transactions on Professional Communication*, Vol. 32, No. 4.

# 4

## CONSUMER DECISION MAKING, INFORMATION NEEDS, AND COMMUNICATION STRATEGIES

Designing a system that provides consumers with meaningful information about vehicle safety requires understanding how consumers think about automobile safety and how they search for and use information in making automobile purchase decisions. In the first section of this chapter a theoretical framework for understanding how consumers are likely to use information in making major product purchases is provided, and implications for the provision of automotive safety information are drawn. In the following two sections the knowledge from surveys and focus groups concerning how consumers think about automobile safety, how they incorporate safety and other attributes in making automobile purchase decisions, what safety information they would like, and how they search for and use information in the purchase decision process is summarized. In the final section, gaps in the current state of knowledge about consumer decision making and information needs are identified, and the research needed to fill these gaps is described.

### FRAMEWORK FOR UNDERSTANDING MAJOR PRODUCT PURCHASE DECISIONS

Car purchasers are faced with an increasing number of vehicle features and options, which complicate their choices. As discussed in the preceding chapter, automotive safety information is plentiful and available from many sources, though it is sometimes difficult to interpret and not always easy to access. Moreover, car purchase decisions often involve difficult trade-offs, such as those between price, intended use, reliability, and safety. Thus consumers could benefit from better comparative information to help simplify their choices.

## Information Processing Theory of Consumer Choice

The nature of the decision problem, the context, the decision makers, and the available information together determine how and how much information is used in making a choice. To reach consumers, information must be available, provided at the appropriate time, and targeted to the intended audiences (Mazis and Staelin 1982, 4). The attention consumers give to information then depends on (*a*) internal factors, such as whether the information is perceived as helpful in achieving progress toward desired goals and whether it is consistent with their prior beliefs, and (*b*) external factors, which are related to the design and distinctiveness of the message, the intensity of the communication (multimedia, multisensory approaches), and the clarity of the message (absence of competing information) (Mazis and Staelin 1982, 5–7).

## The Decision Problem: Motive and Relevance

Consumers make choices to achieve certain purposes or accomplish certain goals (Bettman 1979, 18). Their motivations, which are influenced by their beliefs and experience, affect both the direction and the intensity of search efforts (Bettman 1979, 18–19). The perceived importance of the task is critical to determining how much time and effort consumers devote to searching for information and comparing options (Bettman et al. 1991, 53). For example, a survey of consumer interest in independent product information (Brobeck 1993) conducted by the Consumer Federation of America (CFA) and the American Association of Retired Persons (AARP) found that consumers had the greatest interest in obtaining information about high-cost products; new cars were at the top of the list. People heed information perceived to be important and relevant to them. Although individual drivers generally consider themselves safer than the average driver, they are concerned about the possibility of the negative consequences of driving, such as being in a crash, getting a ticket, losing one's license, or paying more for insurance (Williams et al. 1995, 123).

The decision context also influences decision making. For example, consumers are likely to select and weight decision attributes differently, and may even make different choices, if they feel accountable to others (e.g., family members) or make the decision jointly (Bettman et al. 1991, 63).

## Decision Maker Attributes

Common cognitive constraints and differences in experience and circumstances influence decision making. Consumers have limits on their ability to use information (Bettman et al. 1991, 57). These cognitive limitations influence how consumers search for information, how they transform and use information to narrow their choices, and how they select among alternatives.

Memory constraints, for example, affect both information search and retention. The processing of new information and the solving of problems are constrained by short-term or working memory,[1] which holds a finite amount of information in a given format for a short period.[2] This suggests that information should be kept limited, should not require complex transformations, and should be structured in related units that can assist recall (Bettman et al. 1991, 54–55). How people learn new information and how they recall old information are both influenced by the external cues that can activate memory retrieval, prior knowledge and beliefs, and how prior knowledge and beliefs are organized in long-term memory (Bettman et al. 1991, 57).[3]

People use new information within the context of their existing beliefs (Clement 1983; McCloskey 1983).[4] If they know nothing about a topic, the information may be incomprehensible and dismissed. If they hold misconceptions, they may misinterpret new information or ignore it if it does not conform to their preconceptions (Morgan et al. 1992, 2050; Slovic 1987, 281). Beliefs about vehicle safety are likely to be no exception. Because nearly everyone has driven or ridden in a car, nearly all consumers have some knowledge of vehicle safety. But their understanding of what makes a car safe and how to use safety features varies widely and is heavily influenced by their own driving experiences. It follows that provision of accurate information alone is not likely to change beliefs; prior knowledge, beliefs, and the experience consumers bring to a decision have an important effect on the extent of information search undertaken and the way information is interpreted (Bettman et al. 1991, 70–71). Thus, knowing how people think and what they believe about vehicle safety can increase the probability that vehicle safety information will be understood and used as intended (Bostrom et al. 1994, 796).

Once a choice has been made and a product purchased, the outcome will provide the consumer with new information that can affect subsequent choices and the extent of information search for future purchases (Bettman 1979, 35).

## Decision Strategies

Because consumers have limited capacity to use information, they typically use simplifying strategies or rules of thumb, known as heuristics, to help them decide among complex choices (Kahneman et al. 1982; Tversky and Kahneman 1974; Plous 1993). Consumers facing purchase decisions that require comparisons among numerous alternatives, like buying an automobile, tend to use decision strategies that lead to early elimination of alternatives, thereby minimizing complex computations and resolution of difficult trade-offs (Payne 1976 and Lussier and Olshavsky 1979 in Bettman et al. 1991, 63).[5]

Consumers tend to trade off the effort required to obtain and analyze information against the perceived benefit of making a correct decision. They expend less effort when it is less important to be accurate.[6] The more complex the decision problem and the greater the time pressure, the more likely consumers will use simplifying strategies. In such decisions, information is valuable to the extent that it is easy to use and compatible with the question the consumer is attempting to answer (Mazis and Staelin 1982, 11). It follows that the more simplified and summarized safety information is, the larger the potential number of users.

A description of the many types of decision strategies that have been identified empirically is too lengthy for inclusion here,[7] but the choice of strategy has implications for how automotive safety information might be used. Consumers who eliminate alternatives that do not meet satisfactory minimum values on all attributes are likely to desire different information and use information differently than consumers who look first at alternatives with the highest value on some most important attribute.[8]

## Framing New Information

It follows from the preceding discussion that information is most likely to be meaningful to consumers if it is clearly and simply presented and provides them with a frame of reference for comprehending the contents (e.g., rating scales, comparative information on similar products) (Mazis and Staelin 1982, 6, 7).

The way information is framed and presented affects how it is perceived (Fischhoff et al. 1993). For example, people appear to place more importance on negative information (Bettman et al. 1991, 67).[9] The more explicit the information on risk and consequences, such as the likely severity of potential injury, the greater the perceived seriousness of the outcome and the more likely the information will be recalled (Laughery and Brelsford 1991, 123). Thus it is important to frame information so that consumers will perceive it as relevant to their circumstances (Bostrom et al. 1994, 796; Morgan et al. 1992, 2055).

The way information is presented can also influence how it is used. For example, presentation of information in a table comparing automobiles on various attributes, including safety, encourages consumers to make trade-offs between safety and other characteristics. However, if safety and other information are available for only one model on a window sticker, making these comparisons is more difficult.

## Implications for Provision of Vehicle Safety Information

What conclusions can be drawn from theory about designing meaningful consumer automotive safety information? First, because automobile purchases are complex decisions involving comparisons and trade-offs among many attributes, information about vehicle safety should be easy to access and use to ensure that consumers will consider it in their decision making. Information is most useful if it is limited to a few critical items, requires little transformation, helps simplify comparisons among alternatives, and conveys some sense of the certainty and validity of the underlying data.

Second, information use and decision making are influenced by prior beliefs and knowledge. Consumers will use information to the extent that it is perceived as important, relevant, and consistent with their belief structure. Prior beliefs and experience derive from a number of sources, including previous automobile purchases and general familiarity with cars and driving. Thus, it is important to understand what consumers mean by and believe about automobile safety in designing information about vehicle safety.

### AUTOMOBILE PURCHASE DECISIONS AND THE IMPORTANCE OF VEHICLE SAFETY INFORMATION

The National Highway Traffic Safety Administration (NHTSA) first conducted market research on consumer attitudes about automobile purchases and safety information during the mid-1970s and early 1980s in response to its legislative mandate to provide consumer information.[10] In response to a 1991 congressional request the agency conducted focus groups (S.W. Morris & Co. 1993) and a public meeting (NHTSA 1995a) to improve public awareness and user friendliness of the New Car Assessment Program (NCAP), and it held four town meetings around the country to solicit information about consumer attitudes and needs for automotive safety information (NHTSA 1995b). Focus groups and town meetings do not provide systematic information that can be generalized to the population at large, but they offer useful insights. The findings of relevant market research conducted by automobile manufac-turers, the insurance industry, and university researchers are also reported here to the extent that they shed light on what consumers know and believe about automobile safety, how they incorporate vehicle attributes—including safety—in automobile purchasing decisions, and how they might use additional vehicle safety information.

## Consumer Understanding of Vehicle Safety Characteristics

An extensive search of publicly available information about what consumers know and believe about automobile safety yielded sparse results. Information about consumer understanding of what constitutes a "safe" car comes from a 1993 study by Volvo of recent new car buyers in Sweden.[11] When asked to identify the characteristics of a "safe" car, nearly two-thirds of 300 respondents to a telephone questionnaire listed attributes related to the size and weight of the vehicle (e.g., large, robust, stable, and heavy), although it was not possible to isolate the importance of specific features like vehicle weight. The next most frequently mentioned characteristics included driver air bag (39 percent), side-impact protection (36 percent), and antilock brakes (30 percent). These responses, however, could have been biased because several of these vehicle features had been recent topics of public discussion (presentation to study committee by Ingrid Skogsmo, Automotive Safety Centre, Volvo Car Corporation, Nov. 16, 1995). The telephone respondents were also asked to identify safety-related design features that should be mandatory on all vehicles.[12] Side-impact protection, the vehicle safety cage (i.e., a well-protected occupant compartment), antilock brakes, driver air bags, occupant protection in rollovers, shatterproof window glass, and passenger air bags received the highest ranking in that order.

There is little comparable information about what U.S. consumers know and believe about vehicle safety. The available information suggests that vehicle safety is often equated with the presence of specific safety features or technologies. For example, Ford Motor Company's new vehicle buyer survey reported that consumers are interested in whether vehicles have air bags or antilock brakes, but they do not ask about the performance of the equipment or of the vehicle as a whole (NHTSA 1994, 75, 80). When asked about what additional safety information they would like, participants in NHTSA's focus groups mentioned safety features, such as antilock brakes and air bags (S.W. Morris & Co. 1993, 18). However, few mentioned vehicle crash performance or crash test results; almost no one had heard of NCAP; and few outside of the Washington, D.C., area knew that NHTSA is a government agency (S.W. Morris & Co. 1993, 37). Many wanted to know what makes a car safe—the design, the way it is built, or other factors (S.W. Morris & Co. 1993, 44).

The evidence is also limited about the extent to which U.S. consumers understand the relationship between safety and car size and weight. Some participants in NHTSA's focus groups were aware that large, heavy cars provide protection in a crash and were interested in information about the weight of the vehicle and the strength of construction (S.W. Morris & Co. 1993, 18–19). In a survey of prospective new car buyers by the Insurance Institute for Highway Safety (IIHS), older drivers (60 years and above) rated large size as a very important consideration in buying a new car,[13] but it was unclear whether the reason was comfort or safety (Ferguson 1992, 3).

Two laboratory studies examined driver perceptions of the importance of specific mechanical systems (e.g., brakes, lights, and turning signals) on vehicle safety (MacGregor and Slovic 1989; Slovic et al. 1987). Both found quite diverse responses.[14]

## The Automobile Purchasing Decision Process

Data in the public domain concerning how consumers use information, including safety information, in making automobile purchase decisions are also limited. In-depth group interviews[15] conducted as part of a comprehensive study of automobile consumer information for NHTSA (Booz, Allen Applied Research 1976) lend support to a two-stage process of automobile purchasing: first consumers choose a type or class of car (e.g., compact, minivan), then they select a specific make and model from within that class (III-25, III-32). Consumers appear to be most interested in information about car size, price, body style (e.g., station wagon, sports car), and, in some cases, certain makes or manufacturers during the first stage of the process (Booz, Allen Applied Research 1976, D-12).

More recent studies confirm this two-stage process. For example, a survey of new car[16] purchasers found that nearly four-fifths of all consumers had made some decision about the cars they were interested in purchasing (e.g., which manufacturer, which dealer to purchase from) before their first visit to a dealer showroom (Punj 1987, 74, 77). Only 28 percent, however, had decided on a specific make of car (Punj 1987, 77). Another study that involved detailed interviews with salespersons at dealerships[17] found that consumers typically come to the dealership with preferences about body style and car size and views on expected car use, but only a small fraction were knowledgeable about the specific models available (Horowitz and Russo 1989, 393, 395).

If this two-stage model approximates the diagram shown as Figure 4-1, which also encompasses the consumer's initial belief structure, then it has important implications for the provision of vehicle safety information. First, it suggests the need for information at various stages in the decision process—the point at which the consumer starts thinking about purchasing a car, the initial determination of the desired car type, and the final decision about the specific make and model. Second, it suggests the need for different types and levels of information at each stage. For example, a crashworthiness measure that does not allow comparisons across vehicle size categories is likely to be less relevant in the first stage of the decision process.

## Importance of Vehicle Safety as a Purchase Attribute

Considerably more data are available from the extensive market research conducted by the automobile manufacturers on vehicle attributes that influence automobile purchasing decisions. In recent years safety has become a more important attribute in new car purchases. Historical data collected by General Motors (GM) indicate that in 1994 consumers ranked safety 6th out of 38 possible reasons for choosing the new vehicle they purchased over their second-choice vehicle. The data indicate a fairly steady increase in importance of safety

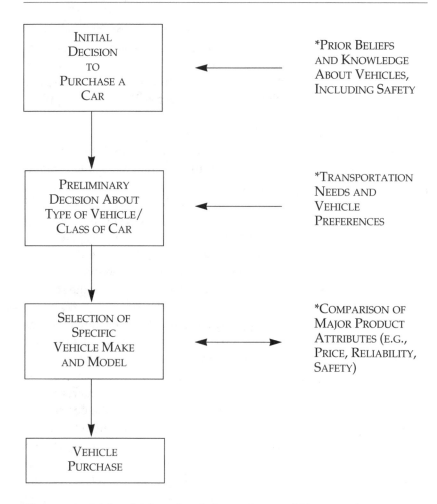

*Points at which vehicle safety information could have an impact

**FIGURE 4-1   Flowchart of two-stage automobile purchase decision process and factors affecting vehicle selection.**

features from 1987, when they ranked 25th (Figure 4-2).[18] In another historical survey (J.D. Power and Associates 1993), prospective car purchasers in 1993 rated "safety in case of accidents" third in importance in selecting a new car, up from fifth 10 years earlier (Figure 4-2).

Although it has grown in importance, safety is still not the most important attribute for most consumers purchasing a new car. Price and

RANKING IN ORDER OF IMPORTANCE

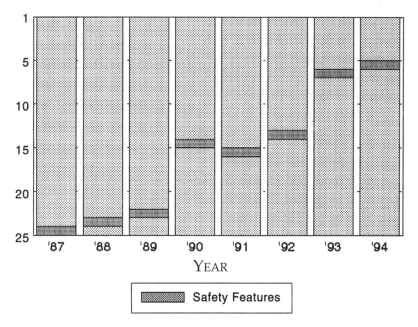

FIGURE 4-2  Changes in the relative importance of safety as a car purchase decision attribute (General Motors Corporation 1994). (New car buyers were asked to rate the three most important items causing them to purchase the car they did rather than their second choice.)

dependability have consistently ranked higher on the average (General Motors Corporation 1994, J.D. Power and Associates 1993). Ford Motor Company's new vehicle buyer study also confirms these results, with safety rated fourth in purchase importance, tied with riding comfort (NHTSA 1994, 74).[19] Another recent survey showed that new car purchasers rated safety features higher on the average than purchasers of pickups, sport utility vehicles, and to a lesser extent vans (Consumer Attitude Research 1994).[20]

One reason that safety may not rank higher in importance is that vehicle safety may be somewhat taken for granted. For example, Ford's buyers survey found that people were generally satisfied with the safety of their automobiles; only 9 out of 32 product attributes were rated higher than safety (NHTSA 1994, 75). Participants in recent NHTSA focus groups stated it more directly: "Safety is not going to be my prime concern because I know that by federal law there are certain features which must be on all vehicles. I trust those features" (S.W. Morris & Co. 1993, 20).

The importance of safety also depends on who is purchasing or using the car. Male participants in the focus groups, for example, noted that while safety was less important than certain other features in cars they drove themselves, it was the most important factor in purchasing a car that will be used by their family (S.W. Morris & Co. 1993, 19). Women tend to rate safety features more highly than men, although the differences are not large.[21] Ford's buyers survey suggests that safety is particularly important for high-income consumers (NHTSA 1994, 75), whereas GM's survey suggests that better-educated consumers rate safety more highly (General Motors Corporation 1994). Finally, owners of larger cars, typically older drivers, also rate safety more highly (J.D. Power and Associates 1993; Consumer Attitude Research 1994). These more safety-conscious market segments are likely to be receptive to improved vehicle safety information and could influence others to use such information.

## Likely Use of Improved Safety Information

Although somewhat dated, the results of 40 group interviews in 1985 with car buyers in four U.S. locations[22] provide an indication of how consumers might use improved vehicle safety information. Respondents suggested that they would use the information primarily in the second stage of their decision process. Once they had narrowed their choices on the basis of such primary criteria as price, vehicle safety information, particularly crashworthiness data, would be used to eliminate the worst-performing cars in the buyer's decision set (National Analysts 1986, 49).[23] In other words, the information would be used as a tie-breaker to help eliminate unsatisfactory alternatives. Better information about the critical relationship between vehicle safety and size and weight could help consumers choose among different types of vehicles (e.g., sport utility vehicles and cars) in the first stage of their decision process and allow them to make trade-offs across product types.

Consumers' perception of driving as a low-risk activity may also affect their receptivity to vehicle safety information. Studies of how lay persons view the risks of various hazardous activities have indicated that motor vehicle crashes are perceived as a familiar, relatively controllable risk similar to risks from fireworks or motorcycles (Slovic 1987, 282). In addition, the relatively low probability of a motor vehicle crash on any one trip is thought to explain why motorists ignore such protective behavior as wearing seat belts despite media campaigns and information that belt use can effectively reduce injury and death in crashes (Slovic et al. 1978, 281). Extending these results to all vehicle safety information, however, is likely to overstate the case. Consumers are apt to be more receptive to safety information related to purchase decisions than to information that requires changes in personal driving habits and behavior. In addition, there is some evidence that motorists' assessment of the riskiness of driving is changing. For example, approximately half the respondents to the IIHS survey reported feeling more risk on the roads today than 5 years ago (Ferguson 1992, 5). Perception of increased risk was particularly notable for older drivers,[24] who are a growing share of the nation's driving population.

## Summary

Marketing data suggest that there is a growing safety-conscious segment of new car purchasers. This group of consumers is likely to be interested in better vehicle safety information. Thus, improved safety information should be targeted to this market segment first.

More information is needed about how to design safety information that will be relevant and useful to this audience. Recent studies and surveys provide limited guidance on how consumers conceptualize vehicle safety. Many consumers appear to equate vehicle safety with the presence of specific safety features, such as air bags and antilock brakes, but have a more limited understanding of other factors that make a car safe. Information is also lacking on how consumers incorporate safety considerations in the overall process of purchasing a car.

To the extent that safety is a factor in automobile purchasing decisions generally, it appears to be used most often to help narrow choices among specific makes and models. The initial choice of type or class of car (e.g., van versus midsized car) appears to be based primarily on price, reliability, and intended use. However, if comparative safety information were available across vehicle classes, it could influence even these initial choices in the long term.

Improvements in the presentation and availability of vehicle safety information could increase general consumer awareness and use of safety information at all stages of the purchase decision process.

## STRUCTURING AND COMMUNICATING VEHICLE SAFETY INFORMATION

### Presentation of Vehicle Safety Information

Summary ratings, which reduce the complexity of processing information about multiple product attributes, can aid the consumer. When asked how vehicle safety information could be presented most effectively, participants in NHTSA's focus groups recommended a standardized measure of the level of safety—a single number or symbol—that could be used to rate all automobiles (S.W. Morris & Co. 1993, 44). Ideally, such a measure could include actual vehicle performance (highway crash statistics) as well as test results (crash tests). It should be expressed in a nontechnical form that could be read and comprehended at a glance by the consumer (S.W. Morris & Co. 1993, 28, 44).

The focus group participants mentioned several models of rating formats, including Environmental Protection Agency (EPA) mileage ratings and appliance energy efficiency ratings (Figures 4-3 and 4-4), that are well liked and readily understood (S.W. Morris & Co. 1993, 44). These ratings provide simple summary measures as well as comparative information, so that consumers can put product-specific information in context. The EPA mileage rating also provides a sense of the certainty of the rating estimate, that is, by how much it is likely to vary with driving habits and vehicle condition.

Because safety is a more complex phenomenon than fuel use or energy efficiency, the design of a summary safety rating or a few summary safety measures is a major challenge. However, focus group respondents clearly believed that some sort of summary measure would be preferable to currently available NCAP data, which represent only a small fraction of real-world crash types (S.W. Morris & Co. 1993, 28, 44).

### Communication of Vehicle Safety Information

Similar to other product ratings, a summary safety rating could be displayed prominently on the product. NHTSA focus group respondents suggested putting the information on all new car labels (S.W. Morris &

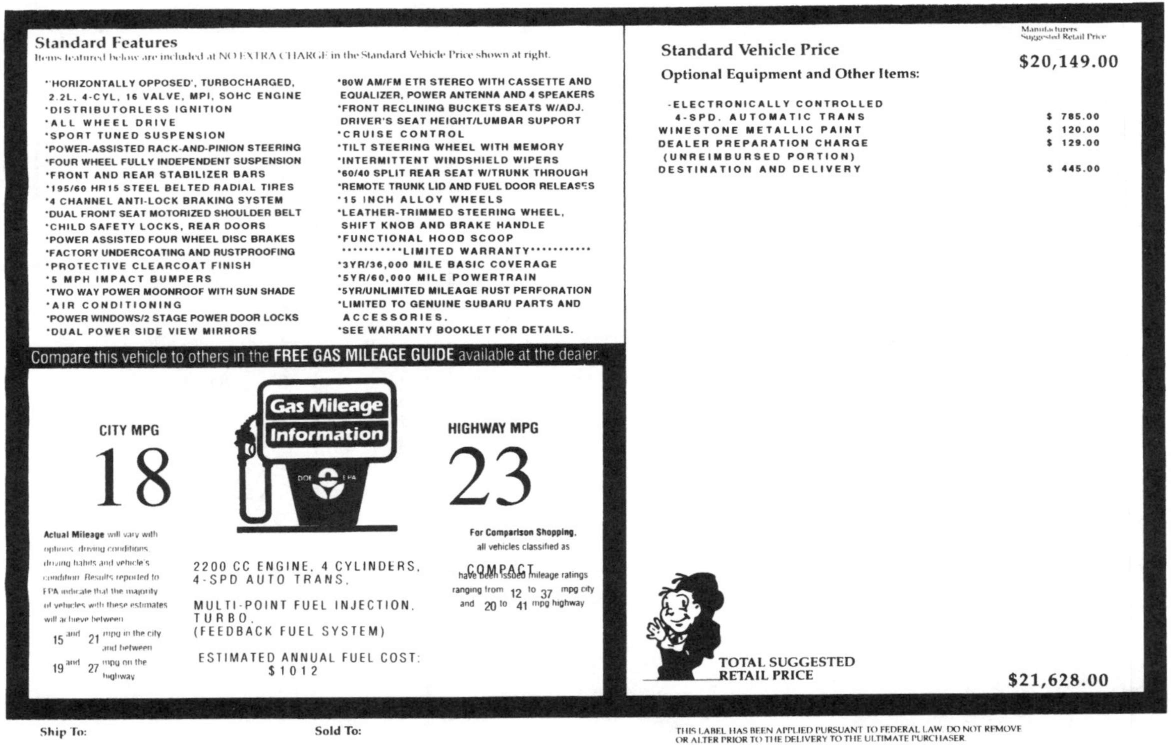

## Standard Features

Items featured below are included at NO EXTRA CHARGE in the Standard Vehicle Price shown at right.

- 'HORIZONTALLY OPPOSED', TURBOCHARGED, 2.2L, 4-CYL, 16 VALVE, MPI, SOHC ENGINE
- DISTRIBUTORLESS IGNITION
- ALL WHEEL DRIVE
- SPORT TUNED SUSPENSION
- POWER-ASSISTED RACK-AND-PINION STEERING
- FOUR WHEEL FULLY INDEPENDENT SUSPENSION
- FRONT AND REAR STABILIZER BARS
- 195/60 HR15 STEEL BELTED RADIAL TIRES
- 4 CHANNEL ANTI-LOCK BRAKING SYSTEM
- DUAL FRONT SEAT MOTORIZED SHOULDER BELT
- CHILD SAFETY LOCKS, REAR DOORS
- POWER ASSISTED FOUR WHEEL DISC BRAKES
- FACTORY UNDERCOATING AND RUSTPROOFING
- PROTECTIVE CLEARCOAT FINISH
- 5 MPH IMPACT BUMPERS
- TWO WAY POWER MOONROOF WITH SUN SHADE
- AIR CONDITIONING
- POWER WINDOWS/2 STAGE POWER DOOR LOCKS
- DUAL POWER SIDE VIEW MIRRORS
- 80W AM/FM ETR STEREO WITH CASSETTE AND EQUALIZER, POWER ANTENNA AND 4 SPEAKERS
- FRONT RECLINING BUCKETS SEATS W/ADJ. DRIVER'S SEAT HEIGHT/LUMBAR SUPPORT
- CRUISE CONTROL
- TILT STEERING WHEEL WITH MEMORY
- INTERMITTENT WINDSHIELD WIPERS
- 60/40 SPLIT REAR SEAT W/TRUNK THROUGH
- REMOTE TRUNK LID AND FUEL DOOR RELEASES
- 15 INCH ALLOY WHEELS
- LEATHER-TRIMMED STEERING WHEEL, SHIFT KNOB AND BRAKE HANDLE
- FUNCTIONAL HOOD SCOOP

**********LIMITED WARRANTY**********

- 3YR/36,000 MILE BASIC COVERAGE
- 5YR/60,000 MILE POWERTRAIN
- 5YR/UNLIMITED MILEAGE RUST PERFORATION
- LIMITED TO GENUINE SUBARU PARTS AND ACCESSORIES.
- SEE WARRANTY BOOKLET FOR DETAILS.

Compare this vehicle to others in the **FREE GAS MILEAGE GUIDE** available at the dealer.

Gas Mileage Information

DOE EPA

CITY MPG

18

HIGHWAY MPG

23

**Actual Mileage** will vary with options, driving conditions, driving habits and vehicle's condition. Results reported to EPA indicate that the majority of vehicles with these estimates will achieve between 15 and 21 mpg in the city and between 19 and 27 mpg on the highway.

2200 CC ENGINE, 4 CYLINDERS,
4-SPD AUTO TRANS.

MULTI-POINT FUEL INJECTION,
TURBO.
(FEEDBACK FUEL SYSTEM)

ESTIMATED ANNUAL FUEL COST:
$1012

**For Comparison Shopping,** all vehicles classified as COMPACT have been issued mileage ratings ranging from 12 to 37 mpg city and 20 to 41 mpg highway

## Standard Vehicle Price

Manufacturers Suggested Retail Price

$20,149.00

**Optional Equipment and Other Items:**

| | |
|---|---|
| -ELECTRONICALLY CONTROLLED 4-SPD. AUTOMATIC TRANS | $ 785.00 |
| WINESTONE METALLIC PAINT | $ 120.00 |
| DEALER PREPARATION CHARGE (UNREIMBURSED PORTION) | $ 129.00 |
| DESTINATION AND DELIVERY | $ 445.00 |

TOTAL SUGGESTED RETAIL PRICE $21,628.00

Ship To:

Sold To:

THIS LABEL HAS BEEN APPLIED PURSUANT TO FEDERAL LAW. DO NOT REMOVE OR ALTER PRIOR TO THE DELIVERY TO THE ULTIMATE PURCHASER.

FIGURE 4-3 Passenger vehicle label with EPA fuel economy ratings.

# ENERGYGUIDE

Refrigerator-Freezer
With Automatic Defrost
With Side-Mounted Freezer
Without Through-the-Door-Ice Service

XYZ Corporation
Model ABC-W
Capacity: 23 Cubic Feet

## Compare the Energy Use of this Refrigerator with Others Before You Buy.

**This Model Uses**
**776**kWh/year

**Energy use (kWh/year) range of all similar models**

**Uses Least**
**Energy**
**776**

**Uses Most**
**Energy**
**1467**

kWh/year (kilowatt-hours per year) is a measure of energy (electricity) use.
Your utility company uses it to compute your bill. Only models with 22.5 to 24.4
cubic feet and the above features are used in this scale.

## Refrigerators using more energy cost more to operate. This model's estimated yearly operating cost is:

**$64**

Based on a 1992 U.S. Government national average cost of 8.25¢ per kWh for
electricity. Your actual operating cost will vary depending on your local utility rates
and your use of the product.

Important: Removal of this label before consumer purchase is a violation of Federal law (42 U.S.C. 6302).

FIGURE 4-4    Energy efficiency label for a major appliance
(*Federal Register* 1994, 148).

Co. 1993, 43). In addition, they recommended an accompanying explanatory page or brochure describing basic facts about the rating measure and how it was calculated.[25] The more detailed information should be written in nontechnical language from the point of view of a prospective car buyer with no special training or expertise in safety engineering or data analysis (S.W. Morris & Co. 1993, 45).

The notion of adding summary information about vehicle safety to other information already available on new car labels is intuitively appealing. Much of the relevant information on purchase attributes would be accessible in one place. However, the amount of information already or soon to be provided on new car stickers—basic information about vehicle features, fuel economy, price, and domestic content[26] (Figure 4-3)—raises the issue of information overload. Research on the effects of information load has produced mixed results,[27] but there is some evidence that label clutter results in diminished information recall (Magat et al. 1988).[28] This suggests that a separate safety label might be more desirable. Consumers would still find price, fuel economy, and information on other important product attributes on the traditional label. Vehicle safety information would be nearby[29] but concentrated on a separate label, thereby not only assisting consumer understanding and recall of vehicle safety information but also emphasizing the importance of safety as a major decision attribute.

The effectiveness of labels as an information medium is the subject of extensive research. Experience with fuel economy and energy efficiency labels suggests that their effectiveness depends on the objective. Longitudinal studies have failed to find evidence that the information provided by labels actually changes purchasing behavior.[30] One could argue, however, that the primary objective of information programs should be to foster more informed decisions (Magat and Viscusi 1992, 185). The studies indicated that the labels increased consumer awareness of energy efficiency and fuel economy as important decision attributes (see text boxes).[31] In addition, labels can motivate the manufacturers to improve their products so that they will receive good ratings on product labels.

Related literature on warning labels and risk communication[32] also provides mixed results on the effectiveness of labels. The evidence for behavior change is weak. For example, one review of studies about warning labels on products such as seat belts, health products, and household chemicals concluded that on-product warnings had no mea-

# FUEL ECONOMY LABELS

The Federal Fuel Economy Information Program was implemented in 1975 under the Energy Policy and Conservation Act. The program has two components—fuel economy labels and a gas mileage guide. The Department of Energy (DOE) is responsible for publication and distribution of the gas mileage guide. DOE, the Environmental Protection Agency (EPA), and the Department of Transportation are jointly responsible for other aspects of the Fuel Economy Information Program, including the fuel economy labels.

The original fuel economy label contained one estimate for fuel economy (combining city and highway driving) and another for annual fuel costs based on projected fuel economy, annual miles driven, and fuel costs. A statement at the bottom of the label referred consumers to a free copy of the gas mileage guide from the dealer, which contained comparative information on the fuel economy of other cars.

In 1981, DOE conducted a major evaluation of the Federal Fuel Economy Information Program (McNutt and Rucker 1981 and Hemphill et al. 1981 in Pirkey et al. 1982). The study was based on a survey of 12,000 model year 1978 and 1979 new car and light truck purchasers and a series of focus groups. DOE found that fuel economy was the single most important factor affecting the purchase of a vehicle. More than 70 percent of purchasers were aware of the fuel economy label, and approximately 50 percent of those aware of the label used it to compare different models (Pirkey et al. 1982, 2). Only about 20 percent of new car purchasers, however, were aware of the gas mileage guide (Pirkey et al. 1982, 2).

Consumers found the original fuel economy labels confusing because one fuel economy number was used on the label, whereas two numbers (i.e., miles per gallon in the city and miles per gallon on the open highway) were used in general advertising. Furthermore, the estimates were not considered credible by consumers. Despite these criticisms, about three-fourths of purchasers believed that the fuel economy ratings, although inaccurate, were useful for making comparisons of vehicle fuel economy (Pirkey et al. 1982, 2).

## FUEL ECONOMY LABELS *(continued)*

A second study was conducted by DOE in 1982 to examine ways to increase the effectiveness and reduce the costs of the Fuel Economy Information Program (Pirkey 1982; Pirkey et al. 1982). Using surveys, focus groups, interviews, literature reviews, and advertising and media reviews, the researchers attempted to determine, among other issues, whether consumer awareness and use of fuel economy labels and consumer attitudes toward fuel economy had changed in the 2 years since new car purchasers had been surveyed. They found that 89 percent of 1981 model year purchasers recognized the label and 63 percent of 1981 model year purchasers used the information provided by the label when making purchase decisions (Pirkey et al. 1982, 4). Moreover, a growing number of purchasers were aware of and used the gas mileage guide before buying a car (Pirkey et al. 1982, 4). It is important to note that, during this time, the importance of fuel economy declined as a major factor influencing new car purchases, in part signaling the end of the energy crises. Price and quality were rated as more important purchase attributes (Pirkey et al. 1982, 4).

The 1982 study found that consumers strongly preferred two fuel economy estimates—one for city and one for highway driving. They also asked for ranges for each estimate for comparable vehicle classes, identification of EPA as the source of the fuel economy estimates (to indicate that they are unbiased), a more positive logo, a more prominent display of the message concerning the availability of the gas mileage guide, and a generally less cluttered label (Pirkey et al. 1982, 8). The fuel economy label was redesigned accordingly on the basis of these findings and recommendations.

Despite the decline in the importance of fuel economy relative to price and quality as a critical new car purchase attribute, consumer awareness and use of the fuel economy label appear to have increased. The fuel economy label was mentioned in surveys as the primary source of consumer information about fuel economy.

## APPLIANCE ENERGY EFFICIENCY LABELS

In December 1975 Congress passed the Energy Policy and Conservation Act (EPCA). One goal was to improve the efficiency of major home appliances through the use of mandated energy labels. EPCA gave the Federal Trade Commission (FTC) responsibility for the establishment of label formats and the Department of Energy "responsibility for a consumer education (persuasion) program to increase the importance of energy information in consumer decisions" (McNeill and Wilkie 1979, 2). The appliance energy labeling program was part of a larger national effort to respond to the energy crisis (McNeill and Wilkie 1979, 1).

In mid-1978 FTC announced tentative label designs, eight of which were implemented nationally in 1980 (i.e., for dishwashers, freezers, refrigerators, refrigerator-freezers, room air conditioners, space heaters, washing machines, and water heaters). The labels included estimates of annual energy costs or efficiency ratings for individual appliances as well as the range for comparable models, and cost grids showing annual operating costs based on utility rates.

Before implementation of the appliance labeling program, McNeill and Wilkie (1979, 9) conducted a laboratory study in which they examined the potential impact of appliance energy labels on consumer purchase decisions and the effect of alternative label formats. They concluded that proposed energy labels appeared to communicate energy performance information well when consumers read them for this purpose. Thus, the labels should increase consumer awareness of and possibly even attitudes toward energy efficiency. There was no objective evidence, however, that they would also affect purchase decisions. In fact, Redinger and Staelin (1980 in Dyer and Maronick 1988, 84) found that consumers tended to treat energy efficiency as they would any other feature (e.g., ice makers and deluxe shelves on refrigerators).

The only longitudinal study on appliance energy label effectiveness (Dyer 1986; Dyer and Maronick 1988), conducted by FTC, included surveys of consumers who had actually purchased appliances both before and 2 and 3 years after the label was introduced. The surveys measured consumer awareness of appliance energy labels and examined changes in the importance consumers attached to energy information. The researchers found that consumer awareness of the energy label and use of energy ef-

## APPLIANCE ENERGY EFFICIENCY LABELS (continued)

ficiency information in purchase decisions increased over time (Dyer and Maronick 1988, 91). However, there was little change in the importance of energy efficiency relative to other product attributes, such as price, size, and warranty (Dyer and Maronick 1988, 89). Awareness of the label itself was related to type of family, age, and previous purchases. For example, two-income households, younger consumers, and first-time buyers were found to have greater awareness of energy information (Dyer and Maronick 1988, 95). The researchers concluded that "appliance energy labeling may have helped introduce energy as an important evaluative criterion for some segments of appliance purchasers" (Dyer and Maronick 1988, 95).

The effectiveness of the energy labeling program depends on the objective being measured. The FTC study did not demonstrate any causal relationship between the labels and increased purchases of energy-efficient appliances (McMahon 1991, 89). However, one could argue that the primary objective of information programs should be to inform consumers. On the basis of that objective, the study indicated that the energy label did increase consumer awareness of energy efficiency as an important purchasing criterion. Because the energy label was implemented in conjunction with a consumer education program, it was not possible to isolate the effects of the label itself.

An amended FTC energy labeling regulation went into effect in December 1994. Labels were revised to be easier for consumers to read and use. Energy labels now feature comparative information about energy use (e.g., usage per year) rather than energy costs, although the latter are still provided as a secondary disclosure. The energy use cost grids were eliminated because they were believed to be confusing to, and rarely used by, consumers; they provided redundant information and detracted from the basic message of the label (*Federal Register* 1994). Both the 1980 and 1994 labels appear to have been well designed: the message is uncluttered and informative—the consumer is given information on a particular product and how it compares with others. However, the new label is simpler.

---

**APPLIANCE ENERGY EFFICIENCY LABELS** (*continued*)

Like the appliance energy label, the automobile safety label will be an informational label that must not be too cognitively demanding on the consumer. The goals of increasing awareness of automobile safety and assisting consumers in making comparative assessments of vehicle safety may be achieved if what is known about label format, structure, and content is used. The label must be uncluttered, readable, and comprehensible. It must also clearly compare the model under consideration with other similar models.

---

surable effect on user behavior or product safety (McCarthy et al. 1984). Other studies that examined consumer responses to warnings of the hazards of chemical products in the home and the workplace found that precautionary behavior did occur, although not universally (Viscusi 1993, 4, 5; Viscusi and Magat 1987, 127). Precautionary actions appeared to be more likely the greater the perceived risk or hazardousness of the product (DeJoy 1989); the greater the congruence between the label information and the consumer's prior belief structure (Adler and Pittle 1984, 166); the more credible (Horst et al. 1986), accurate, and persuasive the information; and the simpler and more informative the communication format (Viscusi and Magat 1987, 126–127; Richardson et al. 1987, 3). Many of these factors, as discussed earlier, would also influence the effectiveness of a vehicle safety label, with one major difference: the objective of hazard warnings is to change behavior, whereas the purpose of information provision is to inform purchase decisions— a less demanding objective.

NHTSA's focus group participants indicated that the credibility of a safety label would be enhanced if the government were clearly identified as the source of the information; information from the automobile companies or other private institutions with a financial interest in automobile safety could not be trusted (S.W. Morris & Co. 1993, 34, 48). A similar recommendation had been made a decade earlier when consumers were asked about their use of the fuel economy label. They suggested that the label should more clearly indicate the federal government as the source of the mileage ratings to assure consumers that the information is impartial and unbiased (Pirkey et al. 1982, 8).

## Matching Dissemination of Vehicle Safety Information with Consumer Information Search Strategies

Research on information search strategies among new car purchasers indicates that the amount of search activity is a function of many variables, including income, education, confidence and experience, satisfaction with previous purchase, and clear idea of product use (Punj 1987, 80). High-search groups tend to be well educated and of high income (Thorelli et al. 1975), although this group can span income categories. They either lack experience with certain product purchases or have not been satisfied with prior purchases (Furse et al. 1984, 423). Low-search groups are experienced, older, have owned more cars on the average, and have been more satisfied with previous purchases than other groups (Furse et al. 1984, 421; Punj and Staelin 1983, 378). Thus various levels of safety information are likely to be required to meet the information needs of potential new car customers.

Consumers not only pursue different information search strategies, but they also need information at different points in the decision process. A well-conceived safety label could provide valuable information at the point of sale. However, consumers engage in considerable information search before they reach the dealership (Punj 1987, 79–80).[33] For example, participants in NHTSA's focus groups indicated that their primary sources of information about new cars were *Consumer Reports*, word of mouth, automobile magazines, and other printed sources such as *The Car Book* (S.W. Morris & Co. 1993, 20). Some consumers had gathered information and had made their decision about which car or type of car to purchase, or at least had narrowed their choices, before even going to the dealer showroom (S.W. Morris & Co. 1993, 18). Thus if information on vehicle safety is to influence consumer choices, it should be made available early in the information search process as well as at the point of sale.

If summary safety ratings are developed, they are likely to be picked up or enhanced by *Consumer Reports* and *The Car Book* and incorporated into the vehicle rating information schemes of these publications. NHTSA's NCAP results have been treated this way. Focus group participants suggested including a toll-free telephone number on the safety rating label that prospective customers could call for additional safety information (S.W. Morris & Co. 1993). The explanatory brochures themselves could provide consumers with relevant safety information, summarized in a single publication, early in the search process. Focus group participants suggested a number of dissemination channels—distribution by insurance companies (along with premium notices), American Automobile Association offices, and departments of motor vehicles, and display at other public locations such as libraries and post offices (S.W Morris & Co. 1993, 24–25). Finally, public service advertisements could help increase consumer awareness of the availability of both the safety label and the related brochures.

## Targeting the Message

Initially it may be most cost-effective to target new vehicle safety information to the audiences that are potentially most receptive. Several such market segments have been suggested in the previous sections, including high-search consumers and the safety conscious. The latter include such groups as families with children, parents of teenage drivers, older drivers, and women.

An effort should also be made to increase general awareness of the importance of vehicle safety to broaden the target audience. One cost-effective way of expediting the diffusion process is to make sure the information is available to "expert" consumers, those shoppers and consumer advocates who have superior skills at interpreting and using consumer information. They can spread the word to other, less expert consumers and help "police" the market by encouraging manufacturers to produce vehicles that receive high safety ratings (Bloom 1989, 171). The effectiveness of this technique depends on the existence of a critical mass of such expert consumers and on the importance of word of mouth as an information source (Bloom 1989, 171). Both conditions appear to be met in the new car sales market.

Another more costly option would be an information campaign on the probability of crashes to motivate more consumers to consider the new safety ratings in purchase decisions. This type of campaign would target motorists who could be persuaded that they are at risk and can effectively reduce that risk through vehicle selection.[34]

## Summary

Determining how best to structure and communicate vehicle safety information is a matter for research. Limited data based largely on NHTSA focus groups suggest that some consumers would find a standardized vehicle safety rating and an accompanying explanatory page or brochure the most effective method of presenting comparative vehicle safety information. Summary measures are attractive because they simplify vehicle comparisons that involve multiple attributes and help focus consumer attention on safety as an important decision criterion. The fuel economy and appliance energy efficiency labels offer good models of understandable, useful summary rating measures.

Similar to other product ratings, a vehicle safety rating could be displayed on a label on all new cars. A separate safety label is probably desirable because of the potential for information overload, given the amount of information placed on existing new car labels. More detailed information explaining the summary rating and its calculation could be made available in a brochure or handbook to accommodate different levels of consumer interest and information processing capabilities.

Vehicle safety information should be introduced at several points in the purchase decision process. A vehicle safety label on all new cars and accompanying explanatory information available at the dealership would provide consumers valuable information near the time of sale. New car purchasers, however, engage in considerable information search and frequently narrow their choices before going to the showroom. Thus, the information should also be made available earlier in the search process.

Not everyone will use vehicle safety information even if it is readily accessible. The most cost-effective way to disseminate the information, at least initially, is to target the most receptive audiences—informed, safety-conscious new car buyers. Public service advertising and education programs are likely to be necessary to create awareness of the availability of the safety information and increase consumer comprehension of the information content, thereby increasing the likelihood of its use.

## RESEARCH NEEDS

Surveys of new car buyers indicate that safety has become a more important factor in new car purchase decisions. These data, however, have been gathered primarily by the automobile manufacturers for market-ing and advertising purposes. Little systematic information is available on what consumers believe or understand about vehicle safety, or how and when they think about safety in choosing a vehicle. Conducting re-search to obtain better information on these topics is an important step in the design of vehicle safety information that consumers will perceive as relevant in their search process.

Determining how vehicle safety information should be presented and introduced into the consumer search process so that consumers will find the information easy to use and available at critical choice points—another important step in improving consumer vehicle safety informa-tion—is also a matter for empirical study. The limited data available suggest that some consumers would like standardized vehicle safety ratings for all passenger vehicles, that the information should be avail-able to inform initial consumer decisions about vehicle class, and that it should be accessible before consumers go to the dealer showroom. These preliminary findings should be confirmed by more systematic re-search. Experimental studies with groups of typical consumers to field test and refine specific communication materials are essential to devel-oping an effective communication strategy.

The research just outlined is a prerequisite for any program to im-prove vehicle safety information. NHTSA should undertake the neces-sary studies, which are neither conceptually difficult nor expensive, without delay.

## NOTES

1. Short- and long-term memory are not thought to be physically distinct en-tities. Rather, short-term or working memory involves the activated por-tion of long-term memory as well as immediate processing and storage of information gathered from the environment (Just and Carpenter 1992 in Byrne 1995; Bettman et al. 1991, 54). Long-term memory is a permanent and unlimited memory store (Bettman et al. 1991, 55; Mazis and Staelin 1982, 10).
2. Working memory, it is said, can handle up to seven plus or minus two meaningful units of information (Miller 1956). However, when competing tasks are involved, working memory capacity may be limited to as few as four to five units of information (Simon 1974).
3. Current theories of memory suggest that long-term memory is organized by (a) causal beliefs, that is, mental models or schemes of how things work; (b) concept categories, which are determined by and related to causal be-

liefs but are also hierarchically related by level of conceptual detail (e.g., vehicle, car, sedan), with the most often used, or basic, concept categories (e.g., car) being easier to understand; and (c) episodes, that is, chronologically organized information about specific experiences and events. Commonly, long-term memory is divided into semantic memory, which includes generic beliefs and categories (a and b) that are not memories of a specific episode or event and episodic memory (c) (Means and Loftus 1991; Tulving 1972).

4. These beliefs are frequently referred to as "mental models," that is, the concepts people use to understand and generate inferences typically about risky choices (Bostrom et al. 1994, 789).

5. These strategies are called noncompensatory, because a poor value on an important attribute typically results in elimination of the alternative. This type of strategy is contrasted with a compensatory approach, which requires trading off high values on some attributes with low values on others in arriving at a final score (Bettman et al. 1991, 60).

6. This cost-benefit perspective has been advanced by Hauser et al. (1993), Punj and Staelin (1983), Bettman et al. (1991), and Russo and Dosher (1983) in Bettman et al. (1991, 64), among others.

7. Some of the more common choice heuristics, which are described by Bettman et al. (1991, 58–60), include the satisficing heuristic (eliminate alternatives if any attribute is below a predetermined cutoff level), the lexicographic heuristic (determine the most important attribute and then examine the values of all alternatives on that attribute), the weighted additive rule (consider and weight all attributes to arrive at an overall evaluation), the elimination-by-aspects heuristic (compare alternatives against the most important attribute and a minimum acceptable value), the majority of confirming dimensions heuristic (compare pairs of alternatives), the frequency of good and bad features heuristic (select the alternative with the highest sum of good features or the lowest sum of bad features), the equal weight heuristic (sum the values of all attributes, which are weighted equally, so the alternative with the largest value is chosen), and the habitual heuristic (select what was chosen the last time).

8. For example, consumers using the former strategy who are provided with vehicle crashworthiness ratings might eliminate certain vehicles from consideration if they did not have a certain minimum score. Consumers using the latter strategy might not consider the crashworthiness information at all unless safety were perceived as an important decision attribute. Therefore, automotive safety information must not only be available, it must be perceived as an important attribute.

9. Prospect theory, which was pioneered by Kahneman and Tversky (1979 in Plous 1993, 95), emphasizes the importance of framing a problem to choices and preferences. It also helps explain how people value and interpret differently decision outcomes that are objectively identical by showing that individuals tend to view outcomes relative to some reference point rather

than as absolute magnitudes and that negative outcomes are counted more heavily than potential gains (Bettman et al. 1991, 65; Plous 1993, 95–101).

10. Title II of the 1972 Motor Vehicle Information and Cost Savings Act (Public Law 92-513) directed NHTSA to conduct a research program to develop information on the damage susceptibility, crashworthiness, repairability, and insurance costs of automobiles for collection and distribution to consumers (Booz, Allen Applied Research 1976, II-1).

11. The study consisted of two parts: (*a*) focus groups of about 50 people were convened to discuss what they considered to be important issues concerning automotive safety; the results of these groups provided the basis for (*b*) a telephone questionnaire of 300 individuals. The respondents were asked to identify the characteristics of a "safe" car (aided question); select which vehicle design features should be mandatory; indicate whether safety information was obtained before car purchase and, if the answer was "yes," from where; and identify the sources of safety information and rate their reliability. Three-fourths of the telephone respondents were male; one-fourth were female. All had purchased one of six new car models in the last 3 months.

12. Respondents were sent a list of 40 items, one item per card, and asked to organize them in order of importance. They were telephoned a second time to obtain the ranking.

13. Thirty-five percent of older drivers (age 60 and above) rated large size as a very important consideration in buying a new car, compared with 23 percent of young drivers (Ferguson 1992, 3).

14. The first study asked subjects to rate 30 motor vehicle subsystems on a set of risk characteristic scales. Drivers gave brakes a high risk rating, which correlated well with crash data that showed brake failures were responsible for the largest proportion of crashes involving vehicular causal factors (MacGregor and Slovic 1989, 386). However, drivers tended to underestimate the importance of communication systems, such as headlights and turning signals, relative to their role in actual crashes (MacGregor and Slovic 1989, 386). The second study (Slovic et al. 1987) also examined individual perceptions of the importance of mechanical systems, such as brakes, steering systems, and fuel lines, to safe vehicle operation. Subjects were asked to evaluate 40 scenarios involving automotive defects on several risk characteristics (e.g., likelihood of damage, injury). Motor vehicle defects were rated widely in terms of their risk characteristics (Slovic et al. 1987, 368).

15. Twelve group interviews were conducted, four in each of three cities. Each group consisted of about eight consumers representing a particular income class and sex (Booz, Allen Applied Research 1976, D-3).

16. The main purpose of the survey was to examine consumer search patterns.

17. The purpose of the study was to develop a conceptual model of a consumer-salesperson interaction to serve as the basis of a computer system that would help consumers select among car sizes, models, and optional features (Horowitz and Russo 1989, 392). Work on this Expert System for

Product Recommendation and Information, which was being developed for General Motors Corporation, has not gone forward.

18. The survey is sent to those who have purchased a vehicle in the past 3 months. It is not limited to those who have purchased a General Motors car.

19. Vehicle durability and reliability, quality, and engine and transmission performance ranked above safety in new vehicle purchases attributes (NHTSA 1994, 74–75).

20. The survey asked respondents to list the two top reasons for purchase among 30 attributes; then, for each attribute, the percentage citing it among the top two reasons was listed. For car purchasers, safety ranked between 4th (for luxury car purchasers) and 10th (for minisubcompact purchasers), with small car purchasers rating safety less high than large car purchasers. Whereas the range for purchasers of light truck vehicles was larger (between 2, for small station wagons, and 18 for mini and small utility vehicles), safety ranked lower, on the average, for purchasers of these types of vehicles (e.g., 13th for standard utility vehicles and 14th and 15th, respectively, for purchasers of small and standard pickups).

21. Slightly more than 14 percent of female respondents versus slightly less than 12 percent of male respondents to the GM survey cited safety features as one of the three most important reasons for purchasing the vehicle they did rather than their second choice (General Motors Corporation 1994). Eleven percent of women versus 9 percent of men rated safety as the third most important feature in selecting a new vehicle (J.D. Power and Associates 1993).

22. Group interviews of eight or nine participants each were conducted during October 1985 in four locations across the United Sates—Portland, Oregon; San Diego, California; Kansas City, Missouri; and Philadelphia, Pennsylvania (National Analysts 1986, 3–5).

23. This response may in part be due to the current focus of crashworthiness information, which provides crash test results for vehicles of similar size.

24. Sixty-three percent of older drivers (age 60 years and above) considered themselves to be more at risk now than 5 years ago compared with only 44 percent of young drivers (age 21 to 29 years) (Ferguson 1992, 5).

25. This is particularly important in the case of a summary measure that represents a weighted average of different product attributes (e.g., car size and weight, crashworthiness in different crash types), where consumers might make different assessments of the relative importance of these attributes.

26. A federal law took effect in late 1994 at the urging of the domestic automobile makers requiring them to put labels on new cars and trucks sold in the United States that identify the foreign-parts content (Lavin 1994). Some manufacturers are providing the information on the current new car label, or Munroney label as it is called. Others are providing a separate label on the window near the Munroney label.

27. Whether information overload occurs and hinders consumer choices remains an important unresolved question in consumer research. A good

summary of the key studies and findings on the information overload question is provided by Magat et al. (1988) and Bettman et al. (1991).

28. A field experiment assessing the impact of different product labels, in this case a hazard warning, on consumers' recall of the information on the labels found that individuals responded to cluttered labels by retaining less of the information, particularly the most important information, on the label (Magat et al. 1988, 230).

29. It may be necessary to display the summary safety information in some other prominent location because of limitations on window space for some vehicles and concerns about visibility in driving test vehicles.

30. A key difficulty was separating the effect of the label from other technological and regulatory changes. For example, technological advances greatly improved the energy efficiency of some major appliances around the time that energy labels were introduced, making it difficult to sort out cause and effect (McMahon 1991, 89).

31. These text boxes were prepared by Beverly Huey, National Research Council staff.

32. Magat and Viscusi (1992), NRC (1989), Richardson et al. (1987), Viscusi and Magat (1987), Hadden (1986), and Morris et al. (1980), among others, are commonly cited.

33. Punj found an inverse relationship between the level of presearch decision making and the amount of external search conducted (measured by the number of dealers consulted and the time spent at these dealers). Consumers who had not made up their minds concerning the manufacturer, brand, or dealer spent a longer time in external search (Punj 1987, 77).

34. This approach is based on protection motivation theory [Rippetoe and Rogers 1987; see also the extended parallel process model proposed by Witte (1992)], a variant of the work on persuasiveness-of-fear appeals. According to the theory, for people to take action to protect themselves, they must first be convinced that they are vulnerable to a threat, that the threat is severe, that there is a clear action for relieving the threat, and that they are capable of taking that action. In the context of automotive safety, the theory implies that consumers must feel that they are at risk of being in a crash, that the crash can be severe, that buying a safer vehicle will help, and that they can buy a safer vehicle. Information on vehicle safety may address the last two (response and self-efficacy) but may not convey that there is a serious, personally relevant threat—the risk of being in a severe crash. An information campaign on the cumulative likelihood of being in different kinds of crashes would be one way of conveying the riskiness of driving and motivating more consumers to attend to safety information.

# References

## Abbreviations

NHTSA    National Highway Traffic Safety Administration
NRC      National Research Council

Adler, R.S., and R.D. Pittle. 1984. Cajolery or Command: Are Education Campaigns Inadequate Substitutes for Regulation? *Yale Journal on Regulation*, Vol. 1, pp. 159–194.

Bettman, J.R. 1979. *An Information Processing Theory of Consumer Choice*. Addison-Wesley Publishing Company, Mass.

Bettman, J.R., E.J. Johnson, and J.W. Payne. 1991. Consumer Decision Making. In *Handbook of Consumer Behavior* (T.S. Robertson and H.H. Kassarjian, eds.), Prentice-Hall, Englewood Cliffs, N.J., pp. 50–84.

Bloom, P.N. 1989. A Decision Model for Prioritizing and Addressing Consumer Information Problems. *Journal of Public Policy and Marketing*, Vol. 8, pp. 161–180.

Booz, Allen Applied Research. 1976. *Final Phase I Report: The Automobile Consumer Information Study, Title II, P.L. 92-513*. DOT-HS-803-254. Bethesda, Md., June, 184 pp.

Bostrom, A., C.J. Altman, B. Fischhoff, and M.G. Morgan. 1994. Evaluating Risk Communications: Completing and Correcting Mental Models of Hazardous Processes, Part II. *Risk Analysis*, Vol. 14, No. 5, pp. 789–798.

Brobeck, S. 1993. *Consumer Desire for Independent Product Information*. Consumer Federation of America and American Association of Retired Persons, Dec., 8 pp.

Byrne, M.D. 1995. *A Computational Theory of Working Memory*. Dissertation proposal. Georgia Institute of Technology, Aug.

Clement, J. 1983. A Conceptual Model Discussed by Galileo and Used Intuitively by Physics Students. In *Mental Models* (D. Gentner and A.L. Stevens, eds.), Lawrence Eribaum Associates, Hillsdale, N.J., Chapter 14.

Consumer Attitude Research. 1994. *Second Quarter Car Study*. Bloomfield Hills, Mich.

DeJoy, D.M. 1989. Consumer Product Warnings: Review and Analysis of Effectiveness Research. In *Human Factors Perspectives on Warnings: Selections from Human Factors and Ergonomics Society Annual Meetings, 1980–1993* (K.R. Laughery, M.S. Wogalter, and S.L. Young, eds.), Human Factors and Ergonomics Society, 1994, pp. 16–20.

Dyer, R.F. 1986. *A Longitudinal Analysis of the Impact of the Appliance Energy Labelling Program*. Office of Impact Evaluation, Federal Trade Commission, Washington, D.C.

Dyer, R.F., and T.J. Maronick. 1988. An Evaluation of Consumer Awareness and Use of Energy Labels in the Purchase of Major Appliances: A Longitudinal Analysis. *Journal of Public Policy and Marketing*, Vol. 7, pp. 83–97.

*Federal Register*. 1994. Final Rule Concerning Disclosures Regarding Energy Consumption and Water Use of Certain Home Appliances and Other Products Required Under the Energy Policy Act. Vol. 59, No. 126, July 1, pp. 34,014–34,067.

Ferguson, S. 1992. *Survey of New Car Buyers*. Insurance Institute for Highway Safety, Arlington, Va., July, 6 pp.

Fischhoff, B., A. Bostrom, and M.J. Quadrel. 1993. Risk Perception and Communication. *Annual Review of Public Health*, Vol. 14, pp. 183–203.

Furse, D.H., G.N. Punj, and D.W. Steward. 1984. A Typology of Individual Search Strategies Among Purchasers of New Automobiles. *Journal of Consumer Research*, Vol. 10, March, pp. 417–431.

General Motors Corporation. 1994. *Continuous Automotive Market Information Program Buyer Behavior*.

Hadden, S.G. 1986. *Read the Label: Reducing Risk by Providing Information*. Westview Press, Boulder, Colo., 257 pp.

Hauser, J.R., G.L. Urban, and B.D. Weinberg. 1993. How Consumers Allocate Their Time When Searching for Information. *Journal of Marketing Research*, Vol. 30, pp. 452–466.

Hemphill, J., et al. 1981. *Impact of Fuel Economy Information on New Car and Light Truck Buyers*. Paper 810779. Society of Automotive Engineers, Warrendale, Pa., June.

Horowitz, A.D., and J.E. Russo. 1989. Modeling New Car Customer-Salesperson Interaction for a Knowledge-Based System. *Advances in Consumer Research*, Vol. 16, pp. 392–398.

Horst, D.P., G.E. McCarthy, J.N. Robinson, R.L. McCarthy, and S. Krumm-Scott. 1986. Safety Information Presentation: Factors Influencing the Potential for Changing Behavior. In *Human Factors Perspectives on Warnings: Selections from Human Factors and Ergonomics Society Annual Meetings, 1980–1993* (K.R. Laughery, M.S. Wogalter, and S.L. Young, eds.), Human Factors and Ergonomics Society, 1994, pp. 86–90.

J.D. Power and Associates. 1993. *Automotive Consumer Profile Study*. Spring.

Just, M.A., and P.A. Carpenter. 1992. A Theory of Comprehension: Individual Differences in Working Memory. *Psychology Review*, Vol. 99, No. 1, Jan., pp. 122–149. Cited in *A Computational Theory of Working Memory* (M.D. Byrne), dissertation proposal, Georgia Institute of Technology, Aug. 1995.

Kahneman, D., and A. Tversky. 1979. Prospect Theory: An Analysis of Decision Under Risk. *Econometrica*, Vol. 47, pp. 263–291.

Kahneman, D., P. Slovic, and A. Tversky (eds.). 1982. *Judgment Under Uncertainty: Heuristics and Biases*. Cambridge University Press, New York.

Laughery, K.R., and J.W. Brelsford. 1991. Receiver Characteristics in Safety Communications. In *Human Factors Perspectives on Warnings: Selections from Human Factors and Ergonomics Society Annual Meetings, 1980–1993* (K.R. Laughery, M.S. Wogalter, and S.L. Young, eds.), Human Factors and Ergonomics Society, 1994, pp. 120–124.

Lavin, D. 1994. New Label Law May Help Consumers Decipher Just How Domestic a Car Is. *Wall Street Journal*, Oct. 3.

Lussier, D.A., and R.W. Olshavsky. 1979. Task Complexity and Contingent Processing in Brand Choice. *Journal of Consumer Research*, Vol. 6, pp. 154–165.

MacGregor, D.G., and P. Slovic. 1989. Perception of Risk in Automotive Systems. *Human Factors*, Vol. 31, No. 4, pp. 377–389.

Magat, W.A., W.K. Viscusi, and J. Huber. 1988. Consumer Processing of Hazard Warning Information. *Journal of Risk and Uncertainty*, Vol. 1, pp. 201–232.

Magat, W.A., and W.K. Viscusi. 1992. *Informational Approaches to Regulation*. MIT Press, Cambridge, Mass., 270 pp.

Mazis, M.B., and R. Staelin. 1982. Using Information-Processing Principles in Public Policymaking. *Journal of Marketing and Public Policy*, Vol. 1, pp. 3–14.

McCarthy, R.L., J.P. Finnegan, S. Krumm-Scott, and G.E. McCarthy. 1984. Product Information Presentation, User Behavior, and Safety. *Proc.*, 28th Meeting of the Human Factors Society, Santa Monica, Calif., pp. 81–85.

McCloskey, M. 1983. Naive Theories of Motion. In *Mental Models* (D. Gentner and A.L. Stevens, eds.), Lawrence Eribaum Associates, Hillsdale, N.J., Chapter 13.

McMahon, J. 1991. Appliance Energy Labeling in the USA. *Consumer Policy Review*, Vol. 1, No. 2, April, pp. 87–92.

McNeill, D.L., and W.L. Wilkie. 1979. Public Policy and Consumer Information: Impact of the New Energy Labels. *Journal of Consumer Research*, Vol. 6, pp. 1–11.

McNutt, B., and E. Rucker. 1981. *Impact of Fuel Economy Information on New Car and Light Truck Buyers*. U.S. Department of Energy, Washington, D.C.

Means, B., and E.F. Loftus. 1991. When Personal History Repeats Itself: Decomposing Memories for Recurring Events. *Applied Cognitive Psychology*, Vol. 5, pp. 297–318.

Miller, G.A. 1956. The Magical Number Seven Plus or Minus Two: Some Limits on Our Capacity for Processing Information. *Psychological Review*, Vol. 63, pp. 81–97.

Morgan, M.G., B. Fischhoff, A. Bostrom, L. Lave, and C.J. Atman. 1992. Communicating to the Public. *Environment, Science, Technology*, Vol. 26, No. 11, pp. 2,049–2,056.

Morris, L.A., M.B. Mazis, and I. Barofsky (eds.). 1980. *Product Labeling and Health Risks*. Banbury Report 6. Cold Spring Harbor Laboratory, Cold Spring Harbor, N.Y.

National Analysts. 1986. *Consumer Attitudes Toward Consumer Information Programs—A Qualitative Report*. DOT-HS-806-947. Booz, Allen & Hamilton, Inc., Philadelphia, Pa., Jan., 123 pp.

NHTSA. 1994. *Transcript of Auto Safety Town Meeting*. Washington, D.C., Oct. 6, 95 pp.

NHTSA. 1995a. *New Car Assessment Program: Public Meeting*. Report to Congress, Feb.

NHTSA. 1995b. *Town Hall Meetings Report*. Office of Public and Consumer Affairs, 13 pp.

NRC. 1989. *Improving Risk Communication*. National Academy Press, Washington, D.C., 332 pp.

Payne, J.W. 1976. Task Complexity and Contingent Processing in Decision Making: An Information Search and Protocol Analysis. *Organizational Behavior and Human Performance*, Vol. 16, pp. 366–387.

Pirkey, D. 1982. *Assessment of the Federal Fuel Economy Information Program*. U.S. Department of Energy, Washington, D.C.

Pirkey, D., B. McNutt, J. Hemphill, and R. Dulla. 1982. *Consumer Response to Fuel Economy Information—Alternative Sources, Uses, and Formats.* Society of Automotive Engineers Technical Paper 820792, Passenger Car Meeting, Troy, Mich., June 7–10, 14 pp.

Plous, S. 1993. *The Psychology of Judgment and Decision Making.* McGraw-Hill, Inc., New York, 302 pp.

Punj, G.N., and R. Staelin. 1983. A Model of Consumer Information Search Behavior for New Automobiles. *Journal of Consumer Research*, Vol. 9, pp. 366–380.

Punj, G. 1987. Presearch Decision Making in Consumer Durable Purchases. *The Journal of Consumer Marketing*, Vol. 4, No. 1, Winter, pp. 71–82.

Redinger, R., and R. Staelin. 1980. An Experimental Investigation of a Consumer's Decision To Buy Energy Efficient Refrigerators. *Proceedings of the International Conference on Consumer Behavior and Energy Use*, S1-30.

Richardson, G.R., A. Rosenthal, C. Hayes, and R. Silver. 1987. *Review of the Research Literature on the Effects of Health Warning Labels.* ADM 281-86-0003. Alcohol, Drug Abuse, and Mental Health Administration, National Institute on Alcohol Abuse and Alcoholism, June.

Rippetoe, P.A., and R.W. Rogers. 1987. Effects of Components of Protection-Motivation Theory on Adaptive and Maladaptive Coping with a Health Threat. *Journal of Personality and Social Psychology*, Vol. 52, No. 3, March, pp. 596–604.

Russo, J.E., and B.A. Dosher. 1983. Strategies for Multiattribute Binary Choice. *Journal of Experimental Psychology: Learning, Memory, and Cognition*, Vol. 9, pp. 676–696.

Simon, H.A. 1974. How Big Is a Chunk? *Science*, Vol. 183, No. 4124, pp. 482–488.

Slovic, P., B. Fischhoff, and S. Lichtenstein. 1978. Accident Probabilities and Seat Belt Usage: A Psychological Perspective. *Accident Analysis and Prevention*, Vol. 10, No. 4, pp. 281–285.

Slovic, P., D. MacGregor, and N.N. Kraus. 1987. Perception of Risk from Automobile Safety Defects. *Accident Analysis and Prevention*, Vol. 19, No. 5, pp. 359–373.

Slovic, P. 1987. Perception of Risk. *Science*, Vol. 236, April 17, pp. 280–285.

S.W. Morris & Co. 1993. *Focus Groups on Traffic Safety Issues: Public Response to NCAP.* DTNH22-90-C-07015. Bethesda, Md., Aug. 23, 51 pp.

Thorelli, H., H. Becker, and J. Engeldow. 1975. *The Information Seekers.* Ballinger, Cambridge, Mass.

Tulving, E. 1972. Episodic and Semantic Memory. In *Organization of Memory* (E. Tulving and W. Donaldson, eds.), Academic Press, New York.

Tversky, A., and D. Kahneman. 1974. Judgment Under Uncertainty: Heuristics and Biases. *Science*, Vol. 185, pp. 1,124–1,130.

Viscusi, W.K., and W.A. Magat. 1987. *Learning About Risk.* Harvard University Press, Cambridge, Mass.

Viscusi, W.K. 1993. *Product-Risk Labeling: A Federal Responsibility.* The AEI Press, Washington, D.C., 74 pp.

Williams, A.F., N.N. Paek, and A.K. Lund. 1995. Factors That Drivers Say Motivate Safe Driving Practices. *Journal of Safety Research*, Vol. 26, No. 2, pp. 119–124.

Witte, K. 1992. Putting the Fear Back into Fear Appeals: The Extended Parallel Process Model. *Communication Monographs*, Vol. 59, No. 4, pp. 329–349.

# 5

## DEVELOPING AND COMMUNICATING NEW MEASURES OF SAFETY

Consumers would benefit from predictive measures of the overall safety performance of new motor vehicles in comparing among purchase choices. Some consumers will also want an explanation of how such summary measures have been developed and more detailed disaggregated information and feature-by-feature comparisons. In this chapter, a strategy for the production and communication of such information is proposed and elaborated.

### ATTRIBUTES OF GOOD SUMMARY MEASURES

Comprehensive measures of vehicle safety performance must meet several requirements. They should

* Be related meaningfully to actual safety for the range of highway conditions in which the vehicle will be operated;
* Provide a summary whose use or interpretation does not require extensive manipulation or combination with other information;
* Be unambiguous and easy to understand and use;
* Convey the degree of uncertainty associated with current knowledge and expert judgment;
* Be transparent and flexible, allowing more sophisticated users to understand how summaries are produced and to apply different judgments to obtain their own summaries when that is desired; and
* Allow the consumer to place the information in context.

The first of these attributes appears obvious. Producing more meaningful measures probably also presents the greatest long-term challenge.

As indicated in Chapter 2, current knowledge can support the production of measures, particularly for crashworthiness, that have some correlation with actual safety performance. The most reliable predictions can probably be achieved through combining crash test results, statistical analysis of real-world crash outcomes, and expert engineering judgment. The resulting predictions will not be perfect, but just as with informed predictions about other uncertain systems, such as the weather, on the average they will be significantly better than guesses.

Consumers are unlikely to have knowledge of the relative frequency with which safety features and characteristics affect crash likelihood or outcomes. Nor are they likely to adequately understand the variability among vehicles in such other key factors as weight and size. For these reasons, predictions of probable vehicle performance in specific crash modes must be placed in the broader context of the relative frequencies of crash modes and the variability in the relative performance of different vehicle types in each crash mode. Detailed comparisons of selected vehicle safety features and characteristics can provide consumers with only a portion of the information they need to make reasoned decisions about safety. Providing them with methods for weighting these features and characteristics by their relative importance would burden consumers with an extremely complex computational task. As discussed in Chapter 4, research suggests that consumers are unlikely to carry out this task and prefer that it be done for them. Hence, the second attribute: to be useful to most people, an ideal measure should provide a summary of overall vehicle safety.

Whether a measure is "unambiguous and easy to understand," the next attribute, is an empirical question. Risk communication research suggests that even experts may not be able to determine how best to explain and communicate a summary measure until they have tested several alternatives with typical consumers (NRC 1989; Roth et al. 1990; Morgan et al. 1992; Bostrom et al. 1994a) using read-aloud protocols (Ericsson and Simon 1993), focus groups (Merton 1956; Merton 1987; Morgan 1988; Stewart and Shamdasani 1990), and other appropriate methods. Conducting a series of such tests and iteratively refining the communications strategy is simple but essential. Without such tests one cannot be certain that a measure whose meaning appears obvious to experts carries the same meaning for laypeople.

For the foreseeable future all estimates of the safety performance of vehicles will involve considerable uncertainty. As noted in Chapter

2, the variability of crash test results based on a single test per vehicle is an important issue. In addition, the types of crash tests available do not adequately represent the wide range of real-world crashes, and crash dummies do not represent the range of human characteristics. Expert judgments involve additional uncertainty. An accurate impression of current knowledge about vehicle performance and safety cannot be conveyed to consumers unless information about the uncertainty associated with the current state of knowledge is given, the fourth attribute.

Such information can be communicated in an easily understood way. The most promising approach is probably some form of graphical representation, such as shaded bars, to indicate a range of values (Ibrekk and Morgan 1987). Two illustrations of how these uncertainties might be portrayed are provided in the next-to-last section of this chapter. The design of any graphics to be used on an actual label should be a matter for empirical investigation. How uncertainty is represented deserves special attention in any such investigation, because the portrayal of uncertainty about a product attribute may reduce its importance in the eyes of the consumer or otherwise alter how it is used in decision making.[1]

Providing consumers with several separate measures of the safety performance of vehicles is of limited value unless guidance is given on how the measures can be combined into a summary assessment. Indeed, consumers are better off with summary measures that simplify comparisons of safety attributes among vehicles and assist decision making. At the same time, consumers should be able to examine the components of any summary measure and have access to a complete description of the weights and other assumptions underlying their combination into a single summary, the fifth attribute.

Placing information in context, the final attribute, involves several factors. A good summary measure should allow comparisons among vehicles. Because a few attributes such as vehicle mass and size can have a profound influence on safety, consumers should be able to compare across vehicle classes as well as among vehicles in the same class. Moreover, they should be able to compare safety information with other important attributes such as price, performance, and reliability.

Because motor vehicle crashes are not the only risks that people face, a vehicle safety information program should also help consumers make meaningful comparisons with other dangers to judge how much attention and how many resources they should allocate to dealing with motor vehicle crash risks.

## DESIGNING EFFECTIVE COMMUNICATIONS

How consumers understand and interpret information depends on what they already know and believe. As explained in Chapter 4, very little research has been done to determine how people frame and think about issues of vehicle safety. Until such research is performed, it is premature to make precise recommendations about the contents of safety messages. The National Highway Traffic Safety Administration (NHTSA) should be able to conduct the necessary initial research fairly quickly (in less than 2 years) and at relatively low cost (for less than $300,000).[2]

An approach that has been used to develop other consumer-oriented risk communications holds promise. The premise is that people have knowledge and beliefs about a topic, which they use to filter and interpret new information (Morgan et al. 1992, 2050; Bostrom et al. 1994a, 789). Communicators need to understand these "mental models" if they are to design messages that will not be dismissed or misinterpreted (Morgan et al. 1992, 2050; Jungerman et al. 1988). The first step is to construct a summary of decision-relevant expert knowledge. This expert knowledge is most usefully represented as a diagram that shows the causal influences among the primary factors affecting the decision at hand. Here the decision involves incorporating safety into a vehicle purchase decision. The next step is to conduct structured, open-ended interviews (Bostrom et al. 1992) of an appropriately selected sample of consumers to elicit their beliefs about the factors that affect the safety of automobiles. Audience segmentation should be taken into account in designing the sampling strategy because some groups, such as new drivers, may differ from others in conceptualizing automobile safety. The interview protocol should allow the expression of both accurate and inaccurate concepts but follow the overall structure of the expert diagram to permit easy comparison with expert knowledge. In-depth interviews are crucial in identifying key beliefs. However, they are also resource-intensive—both time-consuming and difficult to collect and analyze—making it unlikely that this kind of study will be large enough to reliably predict the relative frequency of different beliefs. So in the third stage of the research, the results from the interviews are used to design structured questionnaires, which can be administered to a larger sample of consumers to determine the prevalence of the beliefs encountered in the interviews.

Alternative approaches to studying public understanding of risks differ from the mental models approach primarily in that they do not incorporate an explicit decision-making standard in the form of an expert model. For example, ethnographic interviews conducted by cognitive anthropologists on environmental risks have yielded results similar to those of the mental models approach (Kempton 1991; Kempton et al. 1995; Bostrom et al. 1994b). In another approach, investigators of consumer recall of product use information on household chemical products (Magat et al. 1988) used pretest interviews to develop a checklist of concept categories. Interviewers coded consumers' responses directly into these categories during the interviews. This strategy is less resource intensive but appears less likely to identify systematically the full range of consumer beliefs about a complex risk process. Such studies of public understanding should not be confused with studies of attitudes, opinions, and self-judged levels of knowledge, which are common and do not provide information about the audience's substantive beliefs.

Results from a full-fledged mental models study should be sufficient to support development of a draft vehicle safety message based on both the analysis of the information needed and the assessment of what that audience currently believes. However, experience suggests that appropriate expertise and formative research alone are insufficient to guarantee an effective communication. It is essential to iteratively test any communication empirically using multiple evaluation methods and revise the communication accordingly to ensure that it is effective (Morgan et al. 1992, 2054–2055; Bostrom et al. 1994a, 796).

Different people will want different levels of detail. Some will only want simple summary information. Others will want additional information that explains generally how the summary was developed and provides a broader context for the information. A few will want much greater detail—a tutorial on current knowledge and an elaboration of the expert judgments on which the summary measures are based—so that well-educated consumers, or consumer interest and other groups, can tailor comparisons to their particular needs.

These differences among consumers suggest the need for a hierarchically organized communication strategy. A three-level approach is recommended (Figure 5-1). The first level provides the simplest, most highly summarized information in the form of a vehicle safety label for all new passenger vehicles. More detailed information is provided at the next level down in the hierarchy in the form of a vehicle safety brochure. The brochure would explain in modest detail the fac-

### Level 1: Vehicle Safety Label

The vehicle safety label provides summary information on vehicle crash avoidance and vehicle crash performance.

### Level 2: Vehicle Safety Brochure

The vehicle safety brochure, which is provided in the glove box, explains in modest detail the factors that contribute to crash avoidance and crashworthiness, discusses how these were used to produce the summary measures for the vehicle in question, and might also provide some additional comparisons to other vehicles in the same class.

### Level 3: Safety Handbook

The safety handbook provides a detailed nontechnical explanation of the factors that contribute to vehicle safety, the algorithms used to produce the summary measures, and perhaps several other algorithms and associated results. It will provide detailed comparisons of all vehicles sold in the U.S. market. It will be available in printed form in locations such as libraries, but because much of the specific information will change on a regular basis, it will also be available in computer hypertext at a World Wide Web site that can be visited by consumers, automobile and insurance salespeople, reference librarians, and consumer groups.

**FIGURE 5-1  Proposed hierarchically organized three-level communication strategy. In addition, the information will be available for summary publication by news magazines, consumer organizations, and similar groups.**

tors that contribute to crash avoidance and crashworthiness such as the important role of vehicle size and weight, discuss how these factors were used to produce the summary measures for the vehicle in question, and summarize the detailed information on which the summary measures are based. It might also briefly discuss alternative ways in which the summary information might be generated (e.g., for particular classes of drivers). The vehicle safety brochure would be available in the glove compartment of any new vehicle. As explained in the final section of the chapter, the information it contains would also be available to consumers in various other forms to allow access before they arrive in a showroom.

At the most detailed level in the hierarchy, comparative information for all vehicle size and weight classes would be provided. A printed safety handbook would give a nontechnical but detailed explanation of the factors that contribute to vehicle safety, the algorithms used to produce the summary measures, and perhaps several other algorithms and associated results. It would also include a summary table, listing the safety ratings for all vehicles sold in the U.S. market. At a minimum, the table, if not the entire handbook, should be made available at the dealer showroom. Because much of the information will change on a regular basis, the handbook should also be available in computer hypertext form at a World Wide Web site that can be visited by consumers, automobile and insurance salespeople, reference librarians, and consumer groups. This version might even include software that would allow consumers to generate customized measures tailored to their own needs and driving habits.

## CONTENT OF COMMUNICATIONS

The specific contents of these communications cannot be fully defined until the research on public understanding of vehicle safety that was outlined in the previous section has been completed, but the primary information to be communicated can be identified.

## Development of Summary Safety Ratings

Given a particular driver, road, and traffic conditions, the overall safety of a vehicle depends on how well safety features help prevent a crash and how well the vehicle performs during a crash. Thus summary measures of both crash avoidance and crashworthiness are needed to provide consumers with information on the primary vehicle-related factors that affect safety. In producing a single measure for use by the general public, a reasonable starting point is to assume the average driving characteristics of the general population. In the safety brochure or handbook, it might be desirable to provide several additional summary measures for special populations (e.g., older drivers and teenage drivers).[3]

A single overall summary measure is a desirable long-term goal. However, the committee concludes that it is not currently feasible to produce a summary measure that combines *both* crash avoidance and crash performance information. The committee does believe that, if it is supplemented with the judgment of safety experts, current knowledge is sufficient to support the development of a meaningful single summary measure for vehicle crashworthiness and that such a measure could be made significantly more robust in the future if it is coupled with an appropriate program of continuing research (discussed in the next chapter). Whereas a similar summary measure might be produced for crash avoidance, the committee is not persuaded that the current knowledge is sufficient for experts to agree about how this should be done. The main problem is the relatively limited role that vehicle characteristics (versus driving behavior) currently play in predicting crash involvement. Because the effects of crash avoidance features are often small and observable in laboratory settings but not always in the field, it is difficult for the experts to reach agreement on their risk reduction potential.[4] However, all else being equal, consumers will be better off with these safety features than without them. New vehicle technologies developed as part of the Intelligent Transportation Systems program, such as collision avoidance and night vision systems, may increase the importance of safety features in crash avoidance. For the near term, however, a checklist of key crash avoidance features rather than a summary measure must suffice.

This strategy represents a compromise on several of the attributes outlined at the beginning of the chapter. The compromise is necessitated by incomplete current understanding. As knowledge is gained from refinements in testing methods and field crash data through the iterative process described in the next chapter, consideration should be given to adding a summary measure of crash avoidance and, ultimately, to combining the two measures.

There is no unique way to construct a summary measure of the crashworthiness of a vehicle using the data now available or likely to become available in the foreseeable future. Nor can such a measure be constructed on strictly scientific grounds. The judgment of experts is needed to combine the various relevant data into a defensible estimate of vehicle crash performance.

Expert judgment is commonly combined with formal analysis to support decision making under uncertainty. The methods and techniques that have been developed to support such analysis are referred to as decision analysis (Raiffa 1968; Keeney 1982; Von Winterfeldt and Edwards 1986; Watson and Buede 1987). They have been applied in a variety of fields. In introducing the idea of using judgment to automobile safety experts and providing them with a framework for exercising this judgment, the committee found it useful to personalize the problem in the following form:

> Suppose that your daughter has taken up residence in a land that is similar in its technologies, behaviors, and regulations to our own. However, this land has a completely different set of automobile manufacturers and models. Your daughter asks you to help her pick a vehicle that will offer her and her family good crash safety performance. How do you proceed?

Vehicle weight and size are the first things experts typically want to know about. Although they may argue that various other data, such as highway crash fatality statistics and crash test performance information, have less predictive power, they typically want to include such data in the information they will consider in advising their daughters.

The problem reduces to getting safety experts, statisticians, and decision analysts to work together to refine a consensus about the algorithm they would use to advise their daughters. Whereas the committee has concluded that such a subjective combination is possible, choosing the actual algorithm is a matter for extensive research—an effort beyond the limited time and resources of this committee.

Four sets of data should be considered for inclusion in the construction of a summary measure of vehicle crashworthiness. First is the statistical relationship between the size and weight of a vehicle and its crash performance. Second, crash test results for a specific vehicle are available from the automobile manufacturers, NHTSA, and the insurance industry. With regression analysis, statistical relationships between crash test performance and highway crash performance can be established. The correlation coefficients that can be achieved with current test designs are low, which means that the amount of variance that can be explained on the basis of the test data is small, but it is not zero. Faced with making a choice, consumers on the average will be better off by using the crash results in their decision than they will be by ignoring them (and guessing). Combining the size and weight data with available crash test data will require judgment about both the functional form of the algorithm to be used and the values of various weighting coefficients on the basis of factors such as statistical data on the frequency of various crash types.

Third, a number of engineered features (e.g., structure of the occupant compartment, presence of special energy-absorbing components) influence the overall crashworthiness of a vehicle. Sufficient statistical data may not be available to allow a formal incorporation of these factors into the measure, but they can probably be incorporated through the use of expert judgment.

Once a new car model enters the market, the final type of data—actual highway crash performance—begins to accumulate. Methods are available (DeGroot 1970) that will allow the new data to be combined with prior performance estimates in a process known as Bayesian updating. The result is that over time the predictive power of the crash performance estimate can be improved as more real-world performance data are incorporated.[5]

The summary measure that results from this process, even though it will be updated annually, will involve significant uncertainty. Honesty and fairness to both manufacturers and consumers require that this uncertainty be communicated. Otherwise, a very crude estimate with limited predictive power may be misinterpreted by users as a precise indicator of safety. This means that results must always be reported as ranges, preferably in a graphical display.

Once the creation of a summary estimate of vehicle crashworthiness has begun, improvements should become apparent. A number of crash tests, adding to or replacing those now being conducted, are likely to be found that yield greater predictive power. Through the use of advanced "black box" instrumentation added to the computers that are now on board virtually all new vehicles, field crash data might be refined to yield much greater predictive power than is now possible. An institutional strategy and the activities and resources required to support such a process of continuous refinement and improvement are outlined in the next chapter.

## Reporting Safety Ratings

How best to report a summary measure of expected vehicle safety performance is a question that cannot be answered without conducting experimental studies with groups of laypeople. In general, however, some form of graphical display should be used that allows consumers to compare the crashworthiness (and in the future, the crash avoidance potential) of a specific vehicle with all new vehicles on the market as well as with other vehicles in the same class. A comparison with the median of all vehicles on the market is probably best. The mean can be substantially influenced by a few outliers.

The vehicle safety label should provide simple summary graphics. Because some people find graphics confusing and prefer text, the label should also provide a verbal summary of the result and an explanation of the two or three most influential factors. In the interest of simplicity, it probably should not give detailed data on the value of the component variables. Such information would be provided in the safety brochure that accompanies the vehicle.

The algorithm used to produce the summary measure should reflect the behavioral characteristics of the average population of drivers. If the expert panel that produces the measures believes that significantly different algorithms should be used to reflect different types of drivers (e.g., teenage drivers and older drivers), the results should be briefly summarized in the vehicle safety brochure. A complete nontechnical explanation of the algorithms and how they work should be provided in the safety handbook.

As noted earlier, it will not be possible to specify the design or content of the vehicle safety label, the vehicle safety brochure, or the safety handbook until research on consumer knowledge and beliefs has been completed and draft communications have been field tested and iteratively refined. To illustrate how the middle stages of the safety label production process might proceed, two examples of possible vehicle safety labels were developed and received limited testing (Figure 5-2). Resources did not allow for appropriate evaluation and redesign of these labels. However, the preliminary evaluations illustrate how the process of refinement would work.

A structured interview instrument was used to collect read-aloud protocols from a sample of 10 adults in Pittsburgh (see Appendix D).[6] Interviewees were given first one label, then the other, with the order counterbalanced. For each label, the interviewee was asked to provide first impressions of the label, to read through that label aloud saying anything that came to mind, to comment on what he or she liked or disliked about the label, and finally to explain the graphics in the lower half of the label and provide suggestions for improving the label. Last, in-

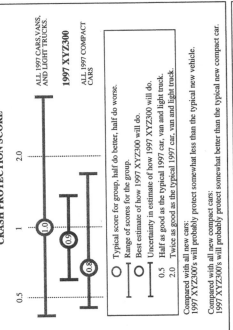

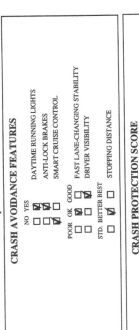

FIGURE 5-2 Examples of possible vehicle safety labels for a hypothetical compact car called the 1997 XYZ300. As discussed in the text, labels must be designed on the basis of experimental studies involving the public. There is no other way to reliably determine what does and does not work.

terviewees were given both labels to compare, then were asked to complete a short written questionnaire (see Appendix D). Each interview lasted 20 to 25 min.

The results of the interviews illustrate the kinds of design guidance such studies can provide and are largely consistent with the focus group study results described in Chapter 4. Interviewees provided suggestions for the arrangement of the graphical display, the composition of the label, and wording or language choices. The comments interviewees made during the read-aloud protocols provide useful insights about several aspects of the label, especially the source of the information on the label, that is, who produced the label; the content of the top statement on safe driving behavior; specific crash avoidance features or the scales used for the features; the graphical crashworthiness displays; the text provided on crashworthiness; and preferences for one label over the other overall, or for some section of one label over that section in the other. Each of these types of comments is discussed in more detail in the following paragraphs.

As in the focus groups, interviewees wanted to know who was responsible for the label and expressed concern that it might have been produced by a manufacturer. Again, this suggests the appropriateness of a clearly indicated government source for vehicle safety information.

Several interviewees made negative comments about the opening statement on driver behavior, referring to it as a "public service commercial" and suggesting that it be dropped or moved. Because driver behavior is a dominant factor, the committee believes that such a statement provides essential information. However, the extensive comments from interviewees suggest that the location and content of any such statement need further study.

Several interviewees did not understand what some of the specific crash avoidance features listed were, such as daytime running lights. Several complained about the use of differing scales. The scale for reporting stopping distance used in the left-hand label was preferred by several respondents, because it made it clear that there was a standard for stopping distance. A few stated that the explanatory text at the top of this section on the left-hand label was helpful.

Almost all the interviewees succeeded in characterizing the graphical displays of crash performance appropriately, if not always completely. Some of the interviewees were able to describe correctly what the graphical display of crash performance was saying after just a brief glance.[7] The modal responses on the written questionnaire showed that interviewees could use the displays to compare the typical values for that specific vehicle with those for its class and for all vehicles and could use the range information for comparative purposes. However, in the interviews the graphical displays were the source of the largest number of comments of all kinds, indicating that interviewees spent most effort on this section of the labels.

Some interviewees called the displays "confusing" and "hard to understand," and some stated that they did not know what the values or scales in the graphics represented. Both positive and negative comments were made about the numbers in the right-hand display. Some interviewees said that they are "nice" and make the display easier to use; others said that they did not know what they mean. Whereas a few interviewees preferred the right-hand display because it was less cluttered, many interviewees stated that they preferred the left-hand label specifically because it provided "the picture explained in text," which they liked. But one interviewee disliked this text as well as the graphical display and spent little time attempting to understand either. He stated emphatically that he did not want to "go to math class to buy this car" and that the comparison is to a "typical car" and not to "anything real." This interviewee did not like the use of qualifying words such as "probably," remarked "no probabilities please," and stated that a description of crash features, such as the "engine will drop down to the ground and not end up in your lap in a crash," would be more useful and had influenced his most recent car purchase.[8]

These interview results alone cannot be generalized, but they illustrate that a graphical display can convey the necessary information to consumers who are concerned about safety. They illustrate the need for additional studies of prior beliefs about vehicle safety and alternative label designs.

Whatever the final design, the content of the safety label should probably not be incorporated into the current vehicle window sticker. A separate label, where all the information relevant to vehicle safety can be concentrated, is desirable. A separate label has a better chance of attracting consumer interest and attention, given the amount of information provided on the existing window label. The safety label should be prominently displayed on the vehicle, but the window may not be the best location because of limitations on window space for some vehicles and concerns about visibility in driving test vehicles.

The design and content of the vehicle safety brochure and the safety handbook should be built on studies of consumer understanding and perception of the determinants of vehicle safety. Once an initial draft has been prepared, it should be subjected to read-aloud protocol analysis (Ericsson and Simon 1993) and other appropriate evaluation (Schriver 1989). As with the safety label, an iterative approach will be essential to produce a communication that is clear and serves consumers' needs.

## GETTING THE MESSAGE OUT

There is no one best way to get vehicle safety information to consumers. The safety label ensures that consumers will have relevant information at the point of sale. The safety brochure and instructions for obtaining it and other information through the NHTSA hotline and electronically via the World Wide Web should be available at the dealer showroom. Dealers could give the brochure and summary information from the handbook to prospective buyers at the same time they provide the NHTSA-required booklet on collision losses. At some stage the latter information might be incorporated into the safety brochure.

The marketing literature clearly indicates that the information should be available to consumers well before they get to the dealer showroom to be most timely and useful. A multichannel approach is recommended. Summary information could be included in selected mailings by insurance companies and organizations such as the American Automobile Association and the American Association of Retired Persons. It could also be advertised, reprinted, or summarized in trade and consumer journals. Portions of the material could be accessed by fax or mail by calling the NHTSA hotline. Finally, the full spectrum of materials should be made available electronically on a hierarchically organized World Wide Web page. To reach younger audiences, a curriculum segment could be developed for use in driver's education courses that explains how to use the safety information in choosing a safe car. Of course, a public service advertising campaign, at least initially, would help increase consumer awareness of the safety label and the accompanying brochures. Once awareness becomes widespread, many safety-conscious consumers can be expected to seek the information at an early stage when they begin to consider purchasing a new car.

These strategies for development and communication of improved vehicle safety information should be viewed as part of a continuing process to yield both improved information and safer cars.

Organizational arrangements for ensuring such a permanent process are considered in the next chapter.

## NOTES

1. Hsee (1995) has found that portrayal of uncertainty for a critical option or attribute (e.g., vehicle safety) can result in a decision maker placing more weight on a less important but more tempting attribute (e.g., vehicle styling).
2. This cost estimate reflects the judgment of several study committee members who have conducted similar research projects.
3. If conditional summary measures of both crash avoidance and crashworthiness could be produced, combining them into a single overall measure would require additional behavioral knowledge as well as an understanding of how those behaviors combine to affect the overall risk of fatality and injury in motor vehicle crashes.
4. Of course, what is known about the crash avoidance potential of vehicle safety features can be made available to consumers in the more detailed safety handbook.
5. Of course, it will not be possible to add this additional information on real-world crash experience when new vehicle models are introduced.
6. The interviews were conducted by Shane Frederick, a Ph.D. student in the Department of Social and Decision Sciences at Carnegie-Mellon University. Interviewees were paid a nominal amount for their participation. All were high school graduates, three had completed college, and two had completed an advanced degree. None were physical scientists or engineers. In comparison, roughly 90 percent of the U.S. population have graduated from high school and almost 25 percent have graduated from college (Rothberg 1995).
7. These interviewees were among the best educated in the sample.
8. Those who preferred the right-hand label were among the more highly educated in the sample. Of those with a high school education, all but this interviewee (who liked neither) preferred the left-hand label with its verbal explanation of the graphics.

## REFERENCES

### Abbreviation
NRC     National Research Council

Bostrom, A., B. Fischhoff, and M.G. Morgan. 1992. Characterizing Mental Models of Hazardous Processes: A Methodology and an Application to Radon. *Journal of Social Issues*, Vol. 48, No. 4, pp. 85–100.

Bostrom, A., C.J. Atman, B. Fischhoff, and M.G. Morgan. 1994a. Evaluating Risk Communications: Completing and Correcting Mental Models of Hazardous Processes, Part II. *Risk Analysis*, Vol. 14, No. 5, pp. 789–798.

Bostrom, A., M.G. Morgan, B. Fischhoff, and D. Read. 1994b. What Do People Know About Global Climate Change? 1. Mental Models. *Risk Analysis*, Vol. 14, No. 6, pp. 959–970.

DeGroot, M. 1970. *Optimal Statistical Decision*. McGraw-Hill, New York.

Ericsson, K.A., and H. Simon. 1993. *Protocol Analysis: Verbal Reports as Data* (revised edition). MIT Press, Cambridge, Mass.

Hsee, C.K. 1995. Elastic Justification: How Tempting but Task-Irrelevant Factors Influence Decisions. *Organization Behavior and Human Decision Processes*, Vol. 62, No. 3, pp. 330–337.

Ibrekk, H., and M.G. Morgan. 1987. Graphical Communication of Uncertain Quantities to Nontechnical People. *Risk Analysis*, Vol. 7, No. 4, pp. 519–529.

Jungerman, H., H. Schutz, and M. Thuring. 1988. Mental Models in Risk Assessment: Informing People About Drugs. *Risk Analysis*, Vol. 8, No. 1, pp. 147–155.

Keeney, R.L. 1982. Decision Analysis: An Overview. *Operations Research*, Vol. 30, No. 5, Sept.–Oct., pp. 803–838.

Kempton, W. 1991. Lay Perspectives on Global Climate Change. *Change*, June, pp. 183–208.

Kempton, W., J.S. Boster, and J.A. Hartley. 1995. *Environmental Values in American Culture*. MIT Press, Cambridge, Mass., 320 pp.

Magat, W.A., W.K. Viscusi, and J. Huber. 1988. Consumer Processing of Hazard Warning Information. *Journal of Risk and Uncertainty*, Vol. 1, pp. 201–232.

Merton, R.K. 1956. *The Focused Interview: A Manual of Problems and Procedures*. Free Press, Glencoe, Ill.

Merton, R.K. 1987. The Focussed Interview and Focus Groups. *Public Opinion Quarterly*, Vol. 51, pp. 550–566.

Morgan, D.L. 1988. *Focus Groups as Qualitative Research*. Sage Publications, Newbury Park, Calif.

Morgan, M.G., B. Fischhoff, A. Bostrom, L. Lave, and C.J. Atman. 1992. Communicating to the Public. *Environment, Science, Technology*, Vol. 26, No. 11, pp. 2,049–2,056.

NRC. 1989. *Improving Risk Communication*. National Academy Press, Washington, D.C., 332 pp.

Raiffa, H. 1968. *Decision Analysis: Introductory Lectures on Choice Under Uncertainty*. Addison Wesley, Reading, Mass.

Roth, E., M.G. Morgan, B. Fischhoff, L. Lave, and A. Bostrom. 1990. What Do We Know About Making Risk Comparisons? *Risk Analysis*, Vol. 10, No. 3, pp. 375–387.

Rothberg, I.C. 1995. Myths About Test Score Comparisons. *Science*, Vol. 270, No. 5241, Dec., pp. 1,446–1,447.

Schriver, K. 1989. Evaluating Text Quality: The Continuum from Text-Focused to Reader-Focused Methods. *IEEE Transactions on Professional Communication*, Vol. 32, No. 4.

Stewart, D.W., and P.N. Shamdasani. 1990. *Focus Groups: Theory and Practice*. Sage Publications, Newbury Park, Calif.

Von Winterfeldt, D., and W. Edwards. 1986. *Decision Analysis and Behavioral Research*. Cambridge University Press, New York.

Watson, S.R., and D.M. Buede. 1987. *Decision Synthesis: The Principles and Practice of Decision Analysis*. Cambridge University Press, New York.

# 6

# ORGANIZATIONAL ARRANGEMENTS

Development of consumer vehicle safety information should be part of an ongoing process to inform the public and provide market and other incentives for the design of safer cars. An organizational structure is needed to sustain these activities and secure the participation of the major interested parties. In this chapter the objectives and functions of such a structure are discussed, organizational options are explored, and an implementation strategy is recommended.

## ORGANIZATIONAL OBJECTIVES

An organizational structure is needed that will support two objectives: (a) creation and dissemination of improved vehicle safety information to assist the general public in making informed choices in the selection of new cars and (b) provision of a process that over time could lead to continuous improvement of the measures used to report vehicle performance and safety.

Any summary measures of crash avoidance and vehicle crashworthiness that can be produced in the next few years will have limited predictive power. If a proposal to produce such measures in the near term is not linked to a broader process that can dramatically improve the predictive power of such measures, it will not adequately serve the long-term interests of the general public, automotive safety regulators, or the automobile industry. Because any measures that can be produced in the next few years would be only loosely correlated with actual vehicle safety performance, they may not provide strong market feedback to encourage improvement in vehicle safety design. Nor would they provide an incentive to improve the crash tests, the crash field data, and the engineering design tools on which the measures are based.

If, instead, the best summary measures that can be produced now are not viewed as a final product but as the first step in designing better measures and safer cars in the future, incentives become apparent. Manufacturers, insurance companies, consumer groups, and others all have an interest in developing and proposing strategies for improvement. An organization charged with developing better measures might conclude that it wants different types of crash tests and different kinds of field crash data than are now available. It might develop advanced statistical strategies to produce a tighter coupling between crash performance in the field and vehicle design and testing. In the longer run, it might even devise a way to develop and use well-calibrated computer-aided design codes to subject all new vehicle designs systematically to a wider range of crash environments than is possible today with a small number of crash tests. Ultimately, under such a system, actual crash tests might be run primarily to ensure good calibration of the computer design codes.

## INSTITUTIONAL CONCEPT AND FUNCTIONS

For the foreseeable future, there appears to be no way to produce meaningful summary measures without exercising considerable expert judgment. For example, crash test data and data accumulated from highway crashes are important in predicting overall vehicle crashworthiness, but they do not tell the whole story. Expert judgment must be exercised to decide how such data should be combined and how to integrate more qualitative factors, such as the presence or absence of specific vehicle safety design features, into the summary predictive measure.

There is no single right way to produce such a measure. From a societal perspective, the best procedure would be to assemble a group of outstanding, economically disinterested automotive experts, statisticians, and decision analysts and give them the independence to construct the best summary measures they can, using all available data and their carefully considered professional judgments. Because short-term market advantages for various automobile companies may depend on the details of these choices, care must be taken so that the experts who propose the measures can make their judgments without undue pressure.

Besides producing the best measures now possible, the group should conduct or commission research to improve the predictive power of such measures. For example, research is needed to devise crash tests that better reflect vehicle performance in real crashes and to ascertain the role of vehicle technologies and their use by drivers in avoiding crashes. The group should have the flexibility to change the measures it uses as better methods become available. It should examine all aspects of the design, testing, and data-gathering process with a view toward developing better predictive measures and producing safer automobiles.

Finally, a group of consumer information specialists, risk perception and risk communication experts, and marketing and advertising professionals should be charged with improving the presentation and dissemination of vehicle safety information. In the short term this could involve improving the presentation of existing disaggregated vehicle safety data and making the data more widely available to consumers early in the automobile purchasing decision process. Once summary safety measures have been developed, dissemination efforts would be focused on communicating these more aggregated data in the ways described in the preceding chapter.

## ORGANIZATIONAL OPTIONS

### Attributes for Effective Operation

A suitable organizational structure should have the following characteristics. First, it must involve the major stakeholders—the National Highway Traffic Safety Administration (NHTSA), the automobile manufacturers selling in the U.S. market, and the insurance industry—who have a direct interest in the outcome of a program to improve consumer vehicle safety information. Safety advocacy and consumer groups should also be broadly represented. The consensus needed to produce and disseminate meaningful consumer vehicle safety information requires the involvement of all the interested parties. Together, they should convene a group of experts in the fields of automotive engineering, highway safety, safety data and statistical analysis, consumer education, risk analysis and communication, marketing, and advertising and charge them with developing the content of a safety information program and dissemination strategies.

Second, the organization must strike a balance between responsiveness and independence. Development of summary safety measures, in particular, will require considerable judgment, and the resulting vehicle ratings may be controversial. Their designers must have the latitude to make judgments independently. At the same time, the designers must be sensitive to the concerns of the stakeholders who are most affected. A balance between independence and responsiveness can probably best be achieved in an environment insulated from direct political influence.

Openness is another important attribute for success. All the assumptions made, alternatives considered, and strategies adopted should be fully described so that they can be subjected to public review and critical evaluation.

Continuity, the fourth organizational attribute, is fundamental to the success of the effort. As discussed previously, significant improvements in consumer safety information and the design of safer vehicles require a continuing commitment supported by a program of long-term research and improvements in crash testing and design procedures.

A related attribute—funding that does not depend entirely on government sources—can help ensure continuity. Meeting long-term objectives requires a multimillion dollar, multiyear effort. Funding from the major stakeholders should help guarantee their continued participation and provide the resources needed to sustain the proposed research program.

Finally, whatever organizational structure is agreed upon, the arrangements must be feasible. Feasibility is broadly defined here to include both political and organizational feasibility.

Whatever organizational arrangement is pursued, success will require cooperation among stakeholders who have different objectives. In the absence of goodwill and strong leadership, no organizational arrangement can guarantee success. Despite the long-term advantages of the system proposed, marketing and other short-term considerations may cause manufacturers to resist a process that will produce sharply focused safety comparisons among motor vehicles. Manufacturers have historically opposed many federal crash test programs, including NHTSA's New Car Assessment Program (NCAP). Such a mind-set may not be easily overcome by promises of long-term improvements. The insurance industry, which has recently instituted a program to develop comparative summary safety information, including offset crash tests, may be reluctant to commit additional financial support to a new safety rating program whose future and success are uncertain. Likewise, NHTSA may find it difficult to join in a cooperative voluntary program while carrying out its other safety-related responsibilities. It is because of such differing concerns and interests that the committee concludes that no organizational arrangement will ensure success without strong and inventive high-level leadership.

## Organizational Alternatives

Five possible institutional arrangements could meet the criteria outlined:

1. Consumer vehicle safety information and dissemination strategies are developed by NHTSA, and the research and plans in support of improved information are produced by NHTSA.
2. The development of consumer vehicle safety information and dissemination strategies is overseen by a NHTSA-appointed advisory committee supported by NHTSA staff and possibly also by outside contractors. Longer-term research and improvements in crash testing and engineering design tools are also overseen by the advisory committee.
3. The functions are managed by a specially chartered private-public organization, which is jointly supported and overseen by NHTSA, the automobile manufacturers selling in the U.S. market, and the insurance industry.
4. The functions are managed by a private-sector group comprising the automobile manufacturers and the insurance industry. They make recommendations to NHTSA about needed research, improved data collection, information dissemination strategies, and changes that should be made in crash test regulations.
5. The functions are handled by one or more nongovernmental organizations (e.g., Consumers Union, the Insurance Institute for Highway Safety, the Society of Automotive Engineers, and the American Automobile Association). They make recommendations for research, data collection, and dissemination strategies that, if adopted by NHTSA and the industry, would promote long-term improvements in consumer vehicle safety information.

### Option 1: Operate Through Existing NHTSA Programs

The first option involves having NHTSA mount the entire undertaking on its own. NHTSA has the authority both to regulate motor vehicles and provide consumer automotive safety information. Agency staff could produce or oversee the production of summary vehicle safety measures. However, NHTSA may have difficulty making, defending, and promulgating the types of judgments that the process requires. Political pressures from direct lobbying and from the executive branch and Congress are inevitable and could threaten the integrity of the program and the stability of other NHTSA programs. In addition, NHTSA may have trouble recruiting and retaining experts with the necessary experience. If some of the work is done by contractors, federal acquisition regulations (e.g., selection of low-cost bids) could make it difficult to employ the best experts.

Once a set of summary safety measures has been developed, if the effort is to lead ultimately to improved methods of crash testing and better vehicle safety designs, NHTSA will find it unproductive to operate entirely on its own. Success requires the participation and cooperation of a number of other parties, especially the manufacturers of motor vehicles. In addition, NHTSA could not undertake such an effort without new funds; securing them will not be easy under todays budgetary constraints. Thus this option violates several of the criteria mentioned at the outset—participation of major stakeholders and relevant experts, adequate insulation from political pressures, broad-based funding, and continuity of effort.

## Option 2: Operate Through a New NHTSA Federal Advisory Committee

The second option involves establishing one or more federal advisory committees supported by NHTSA staff and possibly also by outside contractors. NHTSA has the authority to bring the major stakeholders together in an advisory committee, ensuring the participation of the automobile manufacturers, the insurance industry, and consumer education and safety experts, at least in the short term. The advisory committee structure would ensure balance among the various participants and an open process. It might encourage outside funding. Perhaps most attractive, a federal advisory committee (or committees) could be established rapidly by agency administrative action.[1] The goals of the committee would align well with NHTSA's mission, and the agency could implement its advice directly.

There are drawbacks to this approach. A potential problem is the difficulty of sustaining a substantial research program. With NHTSA in charge, consensus building may be difficult, and industry may not have the incentive to help fund a long-term effort. However, NHTSA's Motor Vehicle Research Safety Advisory Committee has successfully sponsored cooperative public-private research.[2] Although its mission is considerably broader than vehicle safety information, it could provide a model for a new advisory committee with a narrower focus—improving vehicle safety information—and a research agenda.

## Option 3: Create a New Public-Private Automotive Safety Institute

The third option involves the creation of a specially chartered private-public organization—an Automotive Safety Institute (ASI)—jointly supported by NHTSA, the automobile manufacturers selling in the U.S. market, and the insurance industry. The Health Effects Institute (HEI) provides a partial model for such a public-private venture, although other approaches may be appropriate (see text boxes). A board of directors would oversee the development of consumer vehicle safety information and the related research program. The sponsors would operate in an advisory capacity to the board.

---

### THE HEALTH EFFECTS INSTITUTE—A PARTIAL MODEL FOR AN AUTOMOTIVE SAFETY INSTITUTE

Chartered in 1980 as an independent nonprofit corporation, HEI was created to support basic research on the health effects of pollutants from motor vehicles (HEI 1994a, 3). The need for an HEI grew out of an adversarial relationship that had developed between government and industry over air quality regulations. The new institute was to conduct research on regulatory-related issues in a depoliticized environment to improve the science base underlying environmental regulation (T. Grumbly, *The Health Effects Institute: A New Approach To Developing and Managing Regulatory Science*, unpublished manuscript, p. 1).

---

## THE HEALTH EFFECTS INSTITUTE—A PARTIAL MODEL FOR AN AUTOMOTIVE SAFETY INSTITUTE (*continued*)

The U.S. Environmental Protection Agency (EPA) and the manufacturers and marketers of motor vehicles and engines in the United States jointly support HEI's $6 million annual operating budget. EPA and the motor vehicle industry each provide an average of $3 million annually. Industry's share is proportional to the vehicle and engine sales of each of the participating companies (HEI 1994a, 3). To ensure impartiality, however, none of the contributors has control over the research agenda or findings, nor does HEI make recommendations on the regulatory or public policy implications of the research. A board of directors of outstanding scientists, chaired by Archibald Cox, further insulates HEI from political pressure.

The organization has a small, high-quality technical staff, who assist the Institute's Research and Review Committees in overseeing the selection and review of research projects conducted by researchers drawn from across the professional community (HEI 1994b). Since its inception, HEI has funded more than 120 studies and 65 research reports (HEI 1994b, 1).

Creating and sustaining an organization like HEI requires leadership, patience, and a product that is timely and relevant. With the backing of the administrator of EPA, the chairman of General Motors, and its strong board of directors, HEI had the wherewithal to overcome start-up problems. Even with this level of commitment, it took 2 years before any research got under way and 5 years before HEI was operating at nearly full capacity (T. Grumbly, *The Health Effects Institute: A New Approach To Developing and Managing Regulatory Science*, unpublished manuscript, p. 31). Finally, HEI has always walked a fine line between independence and responsiveness to its sponsors. Its sponsors were strong supporters of its mission to conduct high-quality research, but the degree of independence this implied has been difficult to accept in practice. EPA, in particular, has been critical of the relevance and timeliness of HEI's research agenda. Whereas an ASI would probably have a more focused and applied research program, issues of accountability and responsiveness would require careful attention.

## OTHER PUBLIC-PRIVATE MODELS FOR AN AUTOMOTIVE SAFETY INSTITUTE

A recent review of the Health Effects Institute (NRC 1993) suggested that HEI is only one of several models of public-private cooperative ventures. The U.S. Advanced Battery Consortium (USABC), for example, uses the staff and resources of participating organizations. Formed in 1991, USABC is funded equally by the three U.S. automobile manufacturers and the Department of Energy (with some additional funding from the Electric Power Research Institute) to conduct research and development on advanced batteries for electric vehicles (NRC 1993, 106). The sponsoring organizations form committees and make the decisions without separate staff or facilities. USABC has had a more focused technology development program than the more controversial fundamental research program conducted by HEI; by building on existing organizations, its progress has been rapid (NRC 1993, 106).

Another approach is the Partnership for a New Generation of Vehicles (PNGV). In 1993 the U.S. government and the "Big Three" automobile manufacturers committed to a 10-year program to develop a passenger vehicle with up to three times the fuel efficiency of today's midsized sedan but with equivalent performance, safety, and cost (adjusted for economics). One or more prototypes will be developed by 2004. The partnership builds largely on existing resources (redirecting them to PNGV program goals) and personnel in a 50-50 cost-sharing arrangement. The federal government conducts more of the high-risk, fundamental research and the private sector, more of the applied research and development (R&D) (PNGV 1994). A far more complex venture than would likely be required for a consumer automotive safety information program, PNGV illustrates the broad-based support and public-private commitment that are possible for a program with a well-defined goal.

A third public-private partnership founded in 1990—ITS (Intelligent Transportation Systems) America—illustrates the role that a federal advisory committee can play in shaping an R&D program. Since its inception, the board of directors and coordinating council of ITS America have operated as a federal advisory committee to the U.S. Department of Transportation (DOT). Its

---

**OTHER PUBLIC-PRIVATE MODELS FOR AN
AUTOMOTIVE SAFETY INSTITUTE** (*continued*)

role has been to provide policy advice about the general direction of the $100 million to $200 million R&D program at DOT to develop advanced highway and vehicle technologies that could dramatically improve the efficiency of existing highway facilities (TRB 1991). ITS America is organized as a nonprofit organization, receiving one-third of its funds from DOT through a cooperative agreement and two-thirds from private-sector member dues and operations (e.g., annual meeting, publications). With 20 technical committees, its primary mission is to function as an information clearinghouse and coordinating body.

---

This alternative offers several attractions. In contrast to the first two options, it would provide a more neutral environment where experts could work and make judgments relatively insulated from political influence. Because government and industry would be equal partners, an ASI would be more likely to draw private-sector commitment and sustained nongovernmental support. Thus, fewer federal resources might be required in the long term. Finally, the vehicle safety information and research programs would be closely tied in a new organization whose long-term goal would be to integrate crash test and other vehicle safety requirements with the measures used to predict vehicle safety performance. An ASI would have two ongoing programs: (*a*) development of improved consumer vehicle safety information, summary safety measures, and dissemination strategies, and (*b*) research on how to produce better summary safety measures, which would include attention to better vehicle design procedures, crash tests, and crash field data.

The primary drawback of this approach is the difficulty of creating and sustaining a new organization. Any new institution requires leadership, time, and money. Chartering an ASI would require the strong support and funding commitment of the major stakeholders and innovative leadership to weather any start-up difficulties. If the HEI experience is a guide, this option might take longer to produce results. It might also cost more than either of the first two alternatives, but it is likely to yield a more satisfactory long-run outcome. Finally, accountability could become an issue with an independent organization. The charter of an ASI should provide for public as well as professional scrutiny of its programs and products.

## Option 4: Operate Through the Private Sector

Essentially, this would be an industry version of ASI. This option would provide the greatest assurance that programs to improve consumer vehicle safety information would be incorporated into improvements in crash testing and vehicle design. A privately run operation also would not be dependent on uncertain federal support.

Without NHTSA's involvement, however, an industry-only ASI would not be in a strong position to influence changes in crash testing or vehicle safety standards that might be suggested by a long-term program of research. Indeed, without the expectation of future improvement in and possible standardization of vehicle crash test requirements and the measures used to report vehicle safety performance, a key factor motivating industry participation would be lost. Without public involvement, the findings and products of an industry ASI might be viewed as biased and be ignored by the general public.

Alternatively, one or more private organizations could develop summary measures and operate independently but in parallel with a system that involves federal government participation. That could prove beneficial since the more approaches being tested, the greater the likelihood that better strategies will be found and implemented. However, the prospects that any private organization could find the resources to mount such an undertaking are not good.

## Option 5: Operate Through Nongovernmental Organizations

This option has many similarities to the preceding alternative. With public interest groups or professional organizations involved rather than industry alone, the products of this effort have a better chance of being well received by the general public. That being said, this option offers the least potential for bringing together the major stakeholders—NHTSA, the automobile manufacturers, and the insurance industry—to support an integrated program of informational improvements and long-term research leading to improved crash testing methods and safer vehicle designs. Moreover, it is unlikely that consumer groups or professional organizations would have the resources to mount such an endeavor.

## Conclusion

On the basis of the preceding analysis, Options 2 and 3—establishment of a federal advisory committee and creation of a public-private Automotive Safety Institute, respectively—are the most promising. Option 2 would allow the process to start quickly. Convening an advisory committee, developing a plan of action, empaneling a group of experts, and conducting some initial research (i.e., the two projects mentioned in Chapter 4) could probably be accomplished with a modest annual investment of $1 million to $2 million and NHTSA staff support. However, without a congressional mandate, the advisory committee approach might not provide adequate incentives to draw long-term industry support. Option 3 probably offers the best chance of achieving a sustained long-term program, but setting up the proposed ASI is a more difficult undertaking and would take time and a significant investment to produce results.

Although it is premature to provide a definitive estimate, a fully operational program of research, data improvements, vehicle testing, and design initiatives would likely require annual resources on the order of $10 million to $20 million or more under either option, most of which could be expected to come from participating industries.[3]

## IMPLEMENTATION STRATEGY AND NEXT STEPS

Neither organizational approach will work without the cooperation and commitment of both NHTSA and the automobile manufacturers with the largest U.S. sales. The key stakeholders have good reasons to participate. With mission responsibilities for vehicle safety regulation and provision of consumer safety information but limited resources, NHTSA should welcome a broadly funded, market-oriented approach that encourages design and purchase of safer vehicles. The automobile manufacturers would benefit from a program with the potential to improve crash testing programs, particularly if they were to participate in a voluntary effort to develop better testing methods.[4] And, if the information program is successful, that is, if at least some consumers are persuaded to use summary safety ratings in making automobile purchases, it could stimulate demand for new cars with the most advanced designs and safety features. The insurance industry would be motivated to participate because of the long-term potential for the program to reduce customer injury and collision claims.

The Secretary of the Department of Transportation (DOT) should take the first step to bring together the major stakeholders by consulting with senior representatives of the domestic and foreign automobile companies and the insurance industry and with the leadership of the House and Senate appropriations committees who requested this study, to solicit their participation. Congress should follow up this meeting with a formal request and appropriate funding, charging DOT to initiate a process that would lead to the development of summary vehicle safety measures and a mechanism for continuing improvements by 2000. The secretary should determine the most appropriate organizational structure to carry the program forward and issue a progress report within 18 months.

If the process can move forward on a voluntary basis, no new legislative action would be necessary. Once summary safety measures are developed and a few manufacturers start using the labels and the accompanying brochures and booklets, strong pressures would emerge for all manufacturers to participate. Even if some did not, the information would be readily available through other channels (e.g., consumer magazines and the Internet). If, after a few years of experience, a number of manufacturers are still not placing vehicle safety labels on their vehicles and vehicle safety brochures in the glove compartment, labeling and information requirements could be mandated.

## BENEFITS OF CONSUMER VEHICLE SAFETY INFORMATION

Despite improvements in the nations highway safety record, motor vehicle crashes continue to be the leading cause of accidental death in the United States. Improved consumer vehicle safety information can influence consumer choice and manufacturer design of safer vehicles and ultimately reduce the number of fatalities and injuries. However, the magnitude of the safety impact is not known.

Each year, about 15 million new cars, light trucks, vans, and sport utility vehicles are purchased (AAMA 1995, 19, 21). Thus there is a large potential market for understandable comparative information about the safety characteristics of these new vehicles. Widely disseminated summary information could increase awareness of the importance of safety as a purchase attribute and could make it easier for safety-conscious market segments—older drivers, families, and parents of teenage drivers—to comparison shop and select the safest vehicle they can afford. Moreover, it could motivate automobile manufacturers to make improvements in safety design so that their products receive good ratings on summary safety measures.

The value of even a small decline in net fatalities that could be attributed to a consumer automotive safety information program could be considerable and, in the committee's judgment, might easily exceed the costs of supplying better information to consumers and vehicle designers. For example, using current estimates of "willingness to pay" to reduce the risk of deaths from motor vehicle fatalities,[5] a $20 million per year program of research and information would only need to achieve a net mortality reduction on the order of 10 deaths per year[6] to justify program expenditures.

## Notes

1. Although congressional action is not required to establish a federal advisory committee, the agency administrator must register the committee with the appropriate congressional staff. There is also a budget for advisory committees.
2. A recent project involved an assessment of the effectiveness of antilock brakes.
3. This estimate is based on the committee's examination of the budgets of other programs proposed as possible models—HEI and ITS—and the activities to be undertaken.
4. Currently, industry must conduct full-frontal and side-impact crash tests for compliance purposes in the United States; the NCAP test has also become a de facto standard. Offset crash tests are likely to become more common in the future now that the Insurance Institute for Highway Safety has begun its U.S. offset testing program and offset testing standards have been introduced in other markets (e.g., Europe and Australia). The efficiencies to be gained from a more standardized, perhaps even different, set of crash tests should motivate industry participation.
5. Although there has been much controversy in the literature on the treatment of "value of life," most policy analysts have now settled on a willingness-to-pay formulation. Even the term "value of life" is misleading. Nobody is asked to pay this value to avoid a certain death. Rather, this is the implicit marginal rate at which people are prepared to make investments to reduce low-probability mortality risks. A description of the evolution of thinking on these issues can be found in *The Value of Life: An Economic Analysis* (Jones-Lee 1976) and in the first several chapters of *Fatal Tradeoffs: Public and Private Responsibilities for Risk* (Viscusi 1992). The current estimate value of $2.89 million, which the committee used to develop its order-of-magnitude cal-

culation, was produced for the National Safety Council (Fearn et al. 1995, 83). Key elements of these costs were developed by Miller et al. (1991) working under a DOT contract and focusing specifically on motor vehicle applications. It is clear that changes in this value by a factor of two or three will not have a major impact on the qualitative conclusion that is reached.

6. This order of magnitude argument is provided only to give a sense of the magnitude of impact that the program would need to achieve for it to be justified in economic terms. The committee has not performed a detailed benefit-cost or cost-effectiveness calculation. Nevertheless, it believes that in the long run better information for the motor vehicle design process should allow at least some safety improvements to be achieved with little or no change in the real cost of vehicles. A full calculation would need to consider possible increases in vehicle costs and consumer expenditures, the remaining consumer surplus after the incremental safety had been purchased, and possible reductions in the disposable incomes of consumers, which Keeney has pointed out can result in higher risk of mortality (Keeney 1990; Graham et al. 1992). It would also need to consider the possibility that a switch to heavier and larger cars by some consumers in response to a safety information program could have a modest impact on the mortality rates of those still driving lighter and smaller cars. However, it is important to recall that about 60 percent of fatal crashes are single-vehicle crashes and only about one-quarter of fatal crashes involve collisions between passenger vehicles or light trucks (NHTSA 1995, 54–55.) Heavier, larger cars tend to be safer in single-vehicle crashes. Moreover, the weight and size of heavy trucks and buses would not be changed by a program of consumer information.

## REFERENCES

### Abbreviations

| | |
|---|---|
| AAMA | American Automobile Manufacturers Association |
| FHWA | Federal Highway Administration |
| HEI | Health Effects Institute |
| NHTSA | National Highway Traffic Safety Administration |
| NRC | National Research Council |
| PNGV | Partnership for a New Generation of Vehicles |
| TRB | Transportation Research Board |

AAMA. 1995. *Motor Vehicle Facts and Figures*. Detroit, Mich., 96 pp.

Fearn, K.T., L. Kao, and T. Miller. 1995. *Accident Facts, 1995 Edition*. National Safety Council, Itasca, Ill.

Graham, J.D., B. Chang, and J.S. Evans. 1992. Poorer Is Riskier. *Risk Analysis*, Vol. 12, pp. 333–337.

HEI. 1994a. *The Health Effects Institute: An Overview*. Cambridge, Mass., 9 pp.

HEI. 1994b. *HEI Strategic Plan for Vehicle Emissions and Fuels, 1994–1998: Executive Summary*. Cambridge, Mass., Aug., 4 pp.

Jones-Lee, M.W. 1976. *The Value of Life: An Economic Analysis.* University of Chicago Press.

Keeney, R.L. 1990. Mortality Risks Induced by Economic Expenditures. *Risk Analysis*, Vol. 10, pp. 147–159.

Miller, T., J. Viner, S. Rossman, N. Pindus, W. Gellert, J. Douglass, A. Dillingham, and G. Blomquist. 1991. *The Costs of Highway Crashes.* FHWA-RD-91-0555. U.S. Department of Transportation, Oct., 152 pp.

NHTSA. 1995. *Traffic Safety Facts 1994.* DOT-HS-808-292. U.S. Department of Transportation, Aug.

NHTSA and FHWA. 1991. *Moving America More Safely.* U.S. Department of Transportation, Sept., 61 pp.

NRC. 1993. *The Structure and Performance of the Health Effects Institute.* National Academy Press, Washington, D.C., 154 pp.

PNGV. 1994. *Program Plan.* U.S. Department of Commerce, July, 37 pp.

TRB. 1991. *Special Report 232: Advanced Vehicle and Highway Technologies.* National Research Council, Washington, D.C., 90 pp.

Viscusi, W.K. 1992. *Fatal Tradeoffs: Public and Private Responsibilities for Risk.* Oxford University Press.

# Appendix A

## Workshop Agenda and Speakers

### June 21, 1995

### Introductory Remarks

M. Granger Morgan, Head, Department of Engineering and Public Policy, Carnegie-Mellon University (Study Committee Chair)

### Session 1

Motor Vehicle Safety Information Needs and Available Data
Moderator: Tom Gillespie, Director, Great Lakes Center for Truck and Transit Research, The University of Michigan (committee member)

A. Overview of available vehicle safety data
  1. Introduction to motor vehicle safety data and NHTSA's safety data bases
    —Lindsay Griffin, Research Psychologist, Texas Transportation Institute (committee member)
  2. Insurance industry safety data
    —Stephen Oesch, General Counsel, Insurance Institute for Highway Safety

B. Link between safety data and on-road crash experience
  1. NCAP test predictions and frontal crash test results
    —Chuck Kahane, Science Advisor, Plans and Policy, National Highway Traffic Safety Administration
  2. Why doesn't NCAP provide useful consumer information?
    —Ernie Grush, Manager, Accident Statistics and Experiment Design, Ford Motor Company

143

3. New approaches for predicting crashworthiness of new cars
—Forrest Council, Director, Highway Safety Research Center, University of North Carolina
4. Questions and answers

C. Roundtable discussion
1. Questions:
a. How good are currently available safety data?
b. How could existing data be improved to provide meaningful information to consumers?
c. Are there other data that could be used to produce summary measures of crash performance that are not being collected?
2. Participants
George Parker, Vice President, Engineering Affairs, Association of International Automobile Manufacturers
Robert White, Assistant Director, Program Evaluation and Methodology Division, General Accounting Office
Jack Gillis, Director of Public Affairs, Consumer Federation of America
Henry Jasny, Legal Counsel, Advocates for Highway and Auto Safety

## SESSION 2

**Public Perceptions of Highway Safety and Automobile Purchasing Decisions**
**Moderator: Eva Kasten, Executive Vice President, The Advertising Council, Inc., Washington, D.C.**

A. What do we know about the role of information generally, and safety in particular, in consumer car purchase and product use decisions?
1. Results of NHTSA focus groups and town meetings
—Jim Hackney, Director, Office of Market Incentives, National Highway Traffic Safety Administration
2. Car manufacturers buying surveys
—Vann Wilber, Director, Safety and International Technical Affairs, American Automobile Manufacturers Association

—George Parker, Vice President, Engineering Affairs, Association of International Automobile Manufacturers

3. Consumer safety information—a dealer's perspective
—Bob Suddith, Dealer Operator and President, Hoffman Auto Park

4. Questions and answers

B. Effects of consumer information/public education on purchase decisions and product use
1. Effectiveness of public advertising communications
—Theodore Dunn, Technical Consulting Director, Advertising Research Foundation

2. To label or not to label?
—Terry Van Houten, General Engineer, Division of Human Factors, U.S. Consumer Product Safety Commission

3. Effects of energy labels on consumer awareness and use in the purchase of major appliances
—Thomas J. Maronick, Head, Office of Impact Evaluation, Federal Trade Commission

C. Roundtable discussion
1. Question: What more do we need to know about buyer automobile purchasing decisions and the role of safety in those decisions?

2. Participants
Robert Knoll, Testing Director, Auto Test Division, Consumers Union of United States, Inc.

David Van Sickle, Director of Automotive Engineering, American Automobile Association

Diane Steed, President, Coalition for Vehicle Choice

# SESSION 3

**Panel Discussion: Future Directions**
**Moderator: R. David Pittle, Vice President, Technical Director, Consumers Union of United States, Inc. (committee member)**

A. Questions
1. What kinds of safety information do consumers need to know to distinguish a more safe car from a less safe car?

2. How can safety information best be delivered to support informed consumer decision making?
3. Should considerations of safety be made more prominent in the purchase decision process, and, if so, how can this be accomplished?

B. Participants

Leonard Evans, Principal Research Scientist, General Motors Research and Development Center

Philip Haseltine, President, American Coalition for Traffic Safety

Clarence Ditlow, Director, Center for Auto Safety

Paul Bloom, Professor of Marketing, Kenan-Flagler Business School, University of North Carolina

## CONCLUDING REMARKS

**M. Granger Morgan**

# APPENDIX B

## CONGRESSIONAL REQUESTS FOR CONSUMER AUTOMOTIVE SAFETY INFORMATION STUDY, 1994

U.S. Congress, U.S. House of Representatives, Conference Report, H. Rept. 103-752 on H.R. 4556, Making Appropriations for the Department of Transportation and Related Agencies for the Fiscal Year Ending September 30, 1995 and for Other Purposes, Sept. 26, 1994.

*National Academy of Sciences study on automobile labeling.*—The conference agreement includes $300,000 for a study to be conducted by the National Academy of Sciences (NAS) of motor vehicle safety consumer information needs and the most cost effective methods of communicating this information, as proposed by the House. The conferees request that the NAS study include participation from a wide array of experts in marketing, advertising, consumer attitudes, vehicle safety, vehicle product development and manufacturing, as well as consumer representatives and safety advocates. The conferees further request that, as part of its study, the NAS review information gathered by NHTSA through public meetings held in 1994 on the topic of consumer information, and any information gathered by the agency through surveys of occupant protection attitudes, knowledge and behavior. The study should be submitted to the House and Senate Committees on Appropriations no later than March 31, 1996. In order to ensure that the results of the study are considered in the rulemaking process, the conferees agree that NHTSA shall not issue a final regulation concerning motor vehicle safety labeling requirements until after the NAS study is completed.

U.S. Congress, House Committee on Appropriations, H. Rept. 103-543, Part 1, on H.R. 4556, Department of Transportation and Related Agencies Appropriations Act, June 9, 1994.

*National Academy of Sciences study on consumer needs for automobile information.*—The Committee notes that there is increased consumer interest in motor vehicle safety, and recognizes the role that NHTSA can play in assuring that useful information is made available in the most cost effective manner. To some degree, the NCAP addresses this need, but this program is limited in scope and does not necessarily provide a full assessment of a vehicle's overall safety capabilities.

In the Committee's judgment, there is a need for an independent scientific study that considers a broad range of consumer information issues related to motor vehicle safety. Therefore, the Committee has included in the bill $300,000 to support a contract with the National Academy of Sciences for a detailed analysis of motor vehicle safety consumer information needs and the most cost effective methods of communicating this information. This study should be comprehensive in scope, with participation from experts in a variety of areas including marketing, advertising, consumer attitudes, vehicle safety, vehicle product development and manufacturing. The results of the NHTSA public meeting on the NCAP should also be considered in the study process.

The study should focus on the validity of current programs, public and private, in providing accurate information to consumers on the real-world safety of vehicles, the possibility of improving the system in a cost effective and realistic manner, and the best methods of providing useful information to consumers. Through federal and state requirements, vehicles have or will soon have labels providing information on subjects such as fuel economy, domestic content, bumper impact capability, proper placement of child safety seats, the use of safety belts with air bags, as well as price and equipment information. In addition, there is discussion of adding additional safety labeling requirements. Many of the labels provide important information, but questions can be raised about what information is most important to provide and how best to provide that information. The Committee expects these issues to be addressed in the study. Further, the study should address the feasibility of establishing a reliable and effective vehicle rating system.

The study should be submitted to the House and Senate Committees on Appropriations not later than March 31, 1996. The Committee expects that further action by NHTSA on expanding the NCAP to other crash modes and on new safety labeling requirements will be deferred pending the completion of the study.

# APPENDIX C

## FEDERAL MOTOR VEHICLE SAFETY STANDARDS FOR PASSENGER CARS AND LIGHT TRUCK VEHICLES

| STANDARD | REQUIREMENT | APPLIES TO CARS (EFFECTIVE DATE) | APPLIES TO LTVs (EFFECTIVE DATE) |
|---|---|---|---|
| 101 | Identification and illumination of controls and displays | Yes Jan. 1, 1968 | Yes Sept. 1, 1972 |
| 102 | Transmission shift lever sequence | Yes Jan. 1, 1968 | Yes Jan 1, 1968 |
| 103 | Windshield defrosting and defogging | Yes Jan. 1, 1968 | Yes Sept. 1, 1968 |
| 104 | Windshield wiping and washing | Yes Jan. 1, 1968 | Yes Sept. 1, 1968 |
| 105 | Hydraulic brake systems | Yes Jan. 1, 1968 | Yes Sept. 1, 1975 |
| 106 | Brake hoses | a | a |
| 107 | Reflecting surfaces in driver's view | Yes Jan. 1, 1968 | Yes Jan. 1, 1968 |
| 108 | Lamps, reflective devices, and associated equipment | Yes Jan. 1, 1968 | Yes Jan. 1, 1968 |
| 108 | Center high-mounted stop lamp | Yes Sept. 1, 1985 | Yes Sept. 1, 1993 |
| 109 | Tires for use on passenger cars | Yes Jan. 1, 1969 | No |

*(continued on next page)*

## Appendix C  (*continued*)

| Standard | Requirement | Applies to Cars (Effective Date) | Applies to LTVs (Effective Date) |
|---|---|---|---|
| 110 | Tire selection and rims for passenger cars | Yes Sept. 1, 1969 | No |
| 111 | Rearview mirrors | Yes Jan. 1, 1968 | Yes Feb. 12, 1976 |
| 112 | Headlamp concealment devices | Yes Jan. 1, 1970 | Yes Jan. 1, 1970 |
| 113 | Hood latch system | Yes Jan. 1, 1970 | Yes Jan. 1, 1970 |
| 114 | Theft protection | Yes Jan. 1, 1970 | Yes Sept. 1, 1983 |
| 115 | Vehicle identification number | Yes Jan. 1, 1970 | Yes Sept. 1, 1980 |
| 116 | Brake fluid | [b] | [b] |
| 117 | Retreaded tires for use on passenger cars | Yes Jan. 1, 1972 | No |
| 118 | Power windows | Yes Jan. 1, 1972 | Yes Dec. 22, 1988 |
| 119 | New tires for use on vehicles other than passenger cars | No | Yes Sept. 1, 1975 |
| 120 | Tire selection and rims for non-passenger cars | No | Yes Sept. 1, 1976 |
| 121 | Air brake systems | No | No |
| 122 | Motorcycle brakes | No | No |
| 123 | Motorcycle controls and displays | No | No |
| 124 | Accelerator control systems | Yes Sept. 1, 1973 | Yes Sept. 1, 1973 |
| 125 | Warning devices | [c] | [c] |

(*continued on next page*)

## APPENDIX C   (*continued*)

| STANDARD | REQUIREMENT | APPLIES TO CARS (EFFECTIVE DATE) | APPLIES TO LTVs (EFFECTIVE DATE) |
|---|---|---|---|
| 126 | Truck-camper loading | No | Yes Sept. 1, 1973 |
| 129 | Nonpneumatic tires for passenger cars | Yes Sept. 1, 1991 | No |
| 131 | School bus pedestrian safety devices | d | d |
| 201 | Occupant protection in interior impact | Yes Jan. 1, 1968 | Yes Sept. 1, 1981 |
| 202 | Head restraints | Yes Jan. 1, 1970 | Yes Sept. 1, 1991 |
| 203 | Impact protection for the driver from the steering wheel | Yes Jan. 1, 1968 | Yes Sept. 1, 1981 |
| 204 | Steering control rearward displacement | Yes Jan. 1, 1968 | Yes Sept. 1, 1981 |
| 205 | Windows | Yes Jan. 1, 1968 | Yes Jan. 1, 1968 |
| 206 | Door locks and latches | Yes Jan. 1, 1968 | Yes Jan. 1, 1972 |
| 207 | Seating systems | Yes Jan. 1, 1968 | Yes Jan. 1, 1972 |
| 208 | Lap/shoulder belts for front seats, lap belts at all other seats | Yes Jan. 1, 1968 | Yes Jan. 1, 1972 |
| 208 | Lap/shoulder belts at rear outboard seats | Yes Dec. 11, 1989 | Yes Sept. 1, 1991 |

(*continued on next page*)

**APPENDIX C** (*continued*)

| STANDARD | REQUIREMENT | APPLIES TO CARS (EFFECTIVE DATE) | APPLIES TO LTVs (EFFECTIVE DATE) |
|---|---|---|---|
| 208 | Automatic crash protection (either air bags or automatic belts) | Yes Sept. 1, 1989 | Yes Sept. 1, 1997 |
| 208 | Dual air bags and manual lap/ shoulder belt | Yes Sept. 1, 1997 | Yes Sept. 1, 1998 |
| 209 | Seat belts | e | e |
| 210 | Seat belt anchorages | Yes Jan. 1, 1968 | Yes Jan. 1, 1972 |
| 211 | Wheel nuts and hubcaps | Yes Jan. 1, 1968 | Yes Jan. 1, 1968 |
| 212 | Windshield mounting and retention | Yes Jan. 1, 1970 | Yes Sept. 1, 1977 |
| 213 | Child restraint systems | f | f |
| 214 | Side-impact protection— static test | Yes Jan. 1, 1973 | Yes Sept. 1, 1994 |
| 214 | Side-impact protection— crash test | Yes Sept. 1, 1996 | Yes Sept. 1, 1998 |
| 216 | Roof crush test | Yes Aug. 15, 1973 | Yes Sept. 1, 1994 |
| 217 | Bus emergency exits | g | g |
| 218 | Motorcycle helmets | h | h |
| 219 | Windshield intrusion | Yes Sept. 1, 1976 | Yes Sept. 1, 1976 |
| 220 | School bus roll- over protection | d | d |
| 221 | School bus body joint strength | d | d |

(*continued on next page*)

**APPENDIX C** *(continued)*

| STANDARD | REQUIREMENT | APPLIES TO CARS (EFFECTIVE DATE) | APPLIES TO LTVs (EFFECTIVE DATE) |
|---|---|---|---|
| 222 | School bus passenger seating and crash protection | d | d |
| 301 | Fuel system integrity | Yes Sept. 1, 1975 | Yes Sept. 1, 1976 |
| 302 | Flammability of interior materials | Yes Sept. 1, 1972 | Yes Sept. 1, 1972 |
| 303 | Fuel system integrity of compressed natural gas vehicles | Yes Sept. 1, 1995 | Yes Sept. 1, 1995 |
| 304 | Compressed natural gas fuel container integrity | i | i |

Note: Data from National Highway Traffic Safety Administration, 1995.
LTVs = light trucks, vans, and sport utility vehicles.
[a]Not applicable. This is an equipment standard for brake hoses.
[b]Not applicable. This is an equipment standard for brake fluid.
[c]Not applicable. This is an equipment standard for warning devices.
[d]This standard applies only to school buses.
[e]Not applicable. This is an equipment standard that applies to all seat belts regardless of the vehicle in which they are installed.
[f]Not applicable. This is an equipment standard that applies to all child restraints regardless of the vehicle in which they are installed.
[g]This standard applies only to buses.
[h]Not applicable. This is an equipment standard for motorcycle helmets.
[i]This standard applies to all compressed natural gas fuel containers regardless of the vehicle on which the container is installed.

# Appendix D

## Interview Protocol and Questionnaire

### Interview Protocol Used in Evaluating the Two Draft Safety Labels Shown in Figure 5-2

1. Suppose that the government requires that a safety label must be placed on the windows of all new cars sold in the United States. The year is 1997 and you are helping someone shop for a new car. You are looking at a new 1997 compact car called the XYZ300. Here is the label that appears on the window. I'll ask you to read it carefully in a minute, but first, just glance at it quickly and tell me your first impressions.

2. Now, starting right at the top, please read the label to me out loud. As you go along, tell me anything you are thinking, anything at all that comes to mind. Tell me what you like and don't like about the label. What things are clear and understandable? What things do you find confusing, poorly worded?

   *If it gets quiet*: What are you thinking? *or* Please tell me what you're thinking. *or* Talk to me.

   *When they get to the diagrams, if they don't offer it on their own*: Please explain the diagram to me. What is it saying? What is your reaction to it?

3. If you were going to give advice to the people who designed this label, what would you tell them needs work? What changes would you suggest to make the label more useful to the average American car buyer?

4. *Administer the demographic questions.*

5. Here is a different design that might be used for the label on that same compact car, the XYZ300. I'd like you to evaluate it in the same way you did the first one. Start by glancing at it quickly and tell me your first impressions.

6. Now, starting right at the top, please read the label to me out loud. As you go along, tell me anything you are thinking, anything at all that comes to mind. Tell me what you like and don't like about the label. What things are clear and understandable? What things do you find confusing, poorly worded?

   *If it gets quiet*: What are you thinking? *or* Please tell me what you're thinking. *or* Talk to me.

   *When they get to the diagrams, if they don't offer it on their own*: Please explain the diagram to me. What is it saying? What is your reaction to it?

7. Once again, if you were going to give advice to the people who designed this label, what would you tell them needs work? What changes would you suggest to make the label more useful to the average American car buyer?

8. Now here are the two labels together. I'd like you to compare them for me. Tell me which are the best and poorest features of each. If you were going to give the designers some advice for their next label design, what features would you use from each? Are there any things missing that you'd like to see? Are there any things that you think are unnecessary and could be left out?

9. *Administer the written questionnaire.*

## WRITTEN QUESTIONNAIRE USED IN EVALUATING THE TWO DRAFT SAFETY LABELS SHOWN IN FIGURE 5-2

1. Did the labels you saw agree or disagree concerning how safe the 1997 XYZ300 is?

   ___ Agree          ___ Disagree

Please answer the questions below based on the *second* label you looked at:

2. Is the 1997 XYZ300 typically safer than all other 1997 vehicles?

___ Yes ___ No ___ Couldn't tell from label ___ Don't remember

3. Is the 1997 XYZ300 typically safer than all other 1997 compact cars?

___ Yes ___ No ___ Couldn't tell from label ___ Don't remember

4. According to the label, could a 1997 XYZ300 be safer than a typical 1997 car, van, or light truck?

___ Yes ___ No ___ Couldn't tell from label ___ Don't remember

5. Please list the crash avoidance features that were mentioned on the label, and describe the XYZ300 with regard to those features, to the best of your ability.

6. Which crash avoidance feature or features would you pay most attention to if you were purchasing a car?

7. What is the single thing that makes the most difference in determining the risk of an auto accident?

# STUDY COMMITTEE
# BIOGRAPHICAL INFORMATION

**M. Granger Morgan**, *Chairman*, is Head of the Department of Engineering and Public Policy, Professor of Engineering and Public Policy and of Electrical and Computer Engineering, and Professor in the H. John Heinz III School of Public Policy at Carnegie-Mellon University. He received his bachelor's degree in physics from Harvard College, his master's degree in astronomy and space science from Cornell University, and his Ph.D. in applied physics and information science from the University of California at San Diego. Before coming to Carnegie-Mellon, he was a Visiting Associate Physicist at the Brookhaven National Laboratory, and before that he was an Associate Program Director and later Program Director in the Division of Computer Research at the National Science Foundation. Dr. Morgan's research areas include risk assessment and communication, and he has prepared several consumer-oriented publications on such environmental risks as radon, electric and magnetic fields, and global warming and climate change. He is a fellow of the American Association for the Advancement of Science, the Society for Risk Analysis, and the Institute of Electrical and Electronic Engineers. He is a member of the National Research Council Board on Sustainable Development and the recent National Academy of Sciences' Committee on Risk-Related Studies.

**Ann Bostrom** is an Assistant Professor at the School of Public Policy at the Georgia Institute of Technology. She received her M.B.A. at Western Washington University and her Ph.D. in public policy and analysis from Carnegie-Mellon University. Dr. Bostrom's research interests include risk perception and communication, behavioral decision theory, and decision and risk analysis. Before coming to Georgia Tech, she was a Research Associate at the Bureau of Labor Statistics and a Postdoctoral

Research Fellow at Carnegie-Mellon University. She is a member of the American Statistical Association, the Association for Public Policy Analysis and Management, the Society for Judgment and Decision Making, and the Society for Risk Analysis.

**Thomas D. Gillespie** is Director of the Great Lakes Center for Truck and Transit Research at the University of Michigan Transportation Research Institute (UMTRI). Before that, he was a Senior Policy Analyst in the White House Office of Science and Technology Policy, a Research Scientist at UMTRI, a Group Leader of Heavy Truck Engineering at Ford Motor Company, a Research Associate at the Pennsylvania Transportation Institute, a Research Assistant in Mechanical Engineering at Pennsylvania State University, and an Engineer at the Glass Research Center of PPG Industries. Dr. Gillespie received a bachelor of science in mechanical engineering from the Carnegie Institute of Technology and a master's of science and Ph.D. in mechanical engineering from Pennsylvania State University. His professional career has been primarily concerned with advanced engineering and research in the automotive and highway areas. He is a member of the Society of Automotive Engineers and is a registered professional engineer in Pennsylvania.

**Lindsay I. Griffin III** is a Research Scientist at the Texas Transportation Institute (TTI) in the Texas A&M University System. An experimental psychologist, Dr. Griffin received his bachelor of arts in psychology and Ph.D. in experimental psychology from the University of North Carolina. He has held many positions at TTI, including Head of the Safety Division, Head of the Accident Analysis Division, Associate Research Psychologist, Manager of the Traffic Accident Research and Evaluation Programs, and Assistant Research Psychologist. Before that he was Staff Associate at the Highway Safety Research Center at the University of North Carolina and a Teaching Fellow, Teaching Assistant, and Research Assistant in the Department of Psychology. Dr. Griffin is a member of the Association for the Advancement of Automotive Medicine, the American Statistical Association, and the Society of Automotive Engineers. He is Associate Editor of *Accident Analysis and Prevention*. He was the Study Director at the Transportation Research Board for the Committee To Identify Measures that May Improve the Safety of School Bus Transportation.

**Albert I. King** is Distinguished Professor of Mechanical Engineering at Wayne State University and Director of the Bioengineering Center. He also serves as Adjunct Professor of Orthopedics and Associate in Neurosurgery. Dr. King was an Adjunct Professor in the Mechanical Engineering Department at the University of Michigan and, before that, an Assistant, Associate, and Full Professor in the Department of Mechanical Engineering at Wayne State University. He received his bachelor of science from the University of Hong Kong and his master's degree and Ph.D. from Wayne State University. His professional society memberships include the American Society of Mechanical Engineers (Fellow), the Society of Automotive Engineers (Fellow), the American Academy of Orthopedic Surgeons (Associate Member), the American Society of Biomechanics (Member), and the Association for the Advancement of Automotive Medicine (Member). Dr. King also served as a member of the Committee on Trauma Research for the National Academy of Sciences. He is the Associate Editor of the *Journal of Biomechanical Engineering*.

**Wesley A. Magat** is Senior Associate Dean for Academic Programs and Professor at the Fuqua School of Business and Terry Sanford Institute of Public Policy at Duke University. He also directs the program on Regulatory Management at the Center for the Study of Business, Regulation, and Economic Policy. He received his A.B. in mathematics and economics from Brown University and his master's degree and Ph.D. in managerial economics and decision sciences from Northwestern University. Dr. Magat taught as an Associate Professor and Assistant Professor at the Fuqua School of Business. His research interests include the economics of regulation, information regulation, and risk regulation. He is a member of the American Economic Association, the Econometric Society, and the Association for Public Policy Analysis and Management. He also serves on the editorial board of the *Journal of Regulatory Economics*.

**Roger E. Maugh** recently retired after a 37-year career with the Ford Motor Company. Joining Ford in 1957 as a Product Planning Analyst, he held a variety of positions in car and truck planning, marketing, and product development, including Thunderbird Planning Manager, Forward Car Marketing Plans Manager, Ford Car Planning Manager, and Truck Business Planning Manager. He was Assistant Director of Emissions and Fuel Economy Certification, Director of Ford's Automotive Safety Office, Executive Director of Worldwide Automotive Planning, Executive Director of Worldwide Technical Strategy, and most recently, Executive Director of Worldwide Automotive Strategy. Mr. Maugh received his bachelor's degree in mechanical engineering from the University of Michigan, his master's degree in automotive engineering from the Chrysler Institute of Engineering, and his master's degree in business administration from the University of Detroit. He recently completed a term as member of the Intelligent Transportation Society of America Coordinating Council, is a member of the Society of Automotive Engineers, and is a registered professional engineer in Michigan.

**R. David Pittle** is Vice President and Technical Director at Consumers Union of United States, Inc., a position he has held since 1982. In that capacity he oversees all of the product testing, including testing of automobiles, that forms the basis of the product evaluations published in *Consumer Reports*. He received his bachelor of science in electrical engineering at the University of Maryland and his master's of science and Ph.D. in electrical engineering at the University of Wisconsin. Dr. Pittle was Commissioner of the U.S. Consumer Product Safety Commission from 1973 to 1982, an Assistant Professor of Electrical Engineering at Carnegie-Mellon University, an Instructor of Electrical Engineering at the University of Wisconsin, and an Electrical Engineer at the Goddard Space Flight Center. He is a member of the American Association for the Advancement of Science, the Institute of Electrical and Electronic Engineers, the Society for Risk Analysis, the Alliance for Consumer Protection (past President), the Conference of Consumer Organizations, and the Consumer Advisory Panel of Underwriters Laboratories.

**Allan F. Williams** is Senior Vice President for Research at the Insurance Institute for Highway Safety (IIHS), where he also held positions as Senior Behavioral Scientist and Social Psychologist. He received his A.B. in psychology from Wesleyan University and his Ph.D. in social psychology from Harvard University. Before coming to IIHS, Dr. Williams was Project Director at The Medical Foundation, Inc., in Boston, and Alcoholism Research Analyst at the Massachusetts Department of Public Health. He is the author and coauthor of numerous journal articles and publications in the field of highway safety.